Development
and
Social Diversity

Introduced by Mary B. Anderson

A Development in Practice Reader

Series Editor: Deborah Eade

Oxfam (UK and Ireland)

First published by Oxfam UK and Ireland in 1996
Reprinted by Oxfam GB in 1999

© Oxfam UK and Ireland 1999

ISBN 0 85598 343 4

A catalogue record for this publication is available from the British Library.

Available from the following agents:
USA: Stylus Publishing LLC, PO Box 605, Herndon, VA 20172-0605, USA
tel: +1 (0)703 661 1581; fax: + 1(0)703 661 1547; email: styluspub@aol.com
Canada: Fernwood Books Ltd, PO Box 9409, Stn. 'A', Halifax, N.S. B3K 5S3, Canada
tel: +1 (0)902 422 3302; fax: +1 (0)902 422 3179; e-mail: fernwood@istar.ca
India: Maya Publishers Pvt Ltd, 113-B, Shapur Jat, New Delhi-110049, India
tel: +91 (0)11 649 4850; fax: +91 (0)11 649 1039; email: surit@del2.vsnl.net.in
K Krishnamurthy, 23 Thanikachalan Road, Madras 600017, India
tel: +91 (0)44 434 4519; fax: +91 (0)44 434 2009; email: ksm@md2.vsnl.net.in
South Africa, Zimbabwe, Botswana, Lesotho, Namibia, Swaziland:
David Philip Publishers, PO Box 23408, Claremont 7735, South Africa
tel: +27 (0)21 64 4136; fax: +27(0)21 64 3358; email: dppsales@iafrica.com
Tanzania: Mkuki na Nyota Publishers, PO Box 4246, Dar es Salaam, Tanzania
tel/fax: +255 (0)51 180479, email: mkuki@ud.co.tz
Australia: Bush Books, PO Box 1958, Gosford, NSW 2250, Australia
tel: +61 (0)2 043 233 274; fax: +61 (0)2 092 122 468, email: bushbook@ozemail.com.au

Rest of the world: contact Oxfam Publishing, 274 Banbury Road, Oxford OX2 7DZ, UK.
tel. +44 (0)1865 311 311; fax +44 (0)1865 313 925; email publish@oxfam.org.uk

The views expressed in this book are those of the individual contributors, and not necessarily those of the publisher or editor.

Typeset in Gill and Baskerville, printed by Litho & Digital Impressions Ltd (LDi).

Published by Oxfam GB, 274 Banbury Road, Oxford OX2 7DZ, UK
Oxfam GB is a registered charity, no. 202 918, and is a member of Oxfam International.

Contents

Preface

Deborah Eade

Social diversity is a relatively new addition to the lexicon of development practitioners and thinkers. Yet it has quickly come to represent both what is most inspiring, and most depressing, about human potential. The recognition that our needs, our perspectives, and our priorities are shaped both by who we are — and by how we relate to others, and they to us — represents an important advance in our understanding of how societies function. It thus changes how we perceive our own roles, as individuals and as institutions, in working for social and economic justice.

Mary B. Anderson, who introduces this *Development in Practice Reader*, has made major contributions to policy and practice in this field. Her work has provided the international development community with more sensitive tools with which to analyse the contexts within which we act; and more subtle ways in which to listen to those whose thoughts remain unspoken, or whose voices we have been unable (or did not wish) to hear. Her insights into how we can best respond to people's individual *and* collective capacities and vulnerabilities, and specifically in terms of gender analysis, have influenced many official aid agencies and non-governmental organisations (NGOs) around the world.

The greater recognition of social diversity (for instance, in terms of gender, or age, or cultural identity) reveals some of the conflicts *within* social groupings that were previously regarded as homogeneous (such as the household, the urban neighbourhood, or the refugee community). In so doing, it holds up a critical mirror to development processes (and aid programmes), showing how these can actually generate poverty and exclusion. Indeed, the interventions of official agencies and NGOs alike have often exacerbated inequality, and further disempowered the powerless, largely because they have ignored differences in how poverty and oppression are constructed, or the ways in which our identities are mediated by power. Diversity does not mean breaking down society into ever smaller sub-sets, or attaching more labels to people; but rather seeing how the interaction of various aspects of our social and economic identities comes to shape our life options. A deeper understanding of these processes shows how detrimental it can be to trust that the situation of one set of people is a barometer against which to measure the well-being of society as a whole.

Here, Mary B. Anderson argues that the contemporary expressions of intolerance, combined with the extreme abuse of power, require us urgently to re-examine the implications of diversity in the context of development and emergency relief work. The massacres that took place in Rwanda in 1994 were an abhorrent example of how assumed differences between one set of human beings and another can be invoked to inspire acts of unspeakable brutality, and how fear can be manipulated for political and material gain. The cynical term 'ethnic cleansing' disguises barbarity of a similar kind, based on the totalitarian view that difference cannot be accommodated within a society; and, by extension, that belonging to a particular culture or social group means that all individual members must by definition share identical interests. Lethal combinations of fear and loathing have, throughout history, allowed one set of human beings to dehumanise others — emphasising (or inventing) difference in order either to deny the right to express that difference, or (as under the Apartheid regime in South Africa) as a pretext for the systematic subordination of particular communities.

Yet the *denial* of diversity — and hence of the privilege and discrimination that flow from it — can be equally devastating in impairing people's lives. For instance, the 'quiet violence'[1] of the fact that over half of all murders of women, whether in Brazil or in Bangladesh, are committed by their husbands or male partners. Or the 'apartheid of gender',[2] which means that fewer than two dozen women have ever been elected as heads of state or of government in the history of the world. It is the categorisation of people according to a single characteristic or set of traits — a physical disability or illness, skin colour, sex, age, language, political views, sexual orientation, culture or religion — and conceding or denying rights and opportunities to them *on that basis*. When societies believe in their intrinsic fairness — 'in letting the best *man* win' — attempts to redress such systematic bias are often cast as improper interference with the 'natural order', a denial of 'fair play', or an indulgence in 'political correctness'. In addition, certain disciplines and 'laws' are perceived as neutral and immutable. Indeed, discrimination may come to seem so natural that we fail to see it. Yet, after years of research by feminist economists and others, UNDP now estimates that if women's unremunerated (invisible) work was monetised, not only would it yield some US$11 trillion each year, it would irrevocably change the face of orthodox economic analysis.[3] A deeper recognition of the diverse ways in which people relate to the market would thus help to shape development policies in a more equitable way.

Written largely by development practitioners, the papers in this volume demonstrate that we are far from understanding how to create development policies, practices, and institutional mechanisms that can represent (and thus are accountable to) all interests in society, rather than being defined around those of certain privileged or more vocal sectors. But in trying to respond to existing forms of diversity, we must also recognise the wider context in which we are working. For economic globalisation and rapid advances in information technology are generating ever-greater homogeneity across societies and cultures. We listen to the same music, depend on the same computer software, visit the same hamburger chain — and even communicate through the same language — whether we are in Miami, Manila, or Moscow. The challenge is to form the kinds of alliance that are needed in order to resist cultural and ideological domination, but without falling into an anachronistic isolationism.

If we believe in the universality of human rights, an awareness of diversity places upon us a moral responsibility to work for the eradication of the discrimination and exclusion that stem from it. However, such an awareness also holds the promise of still richer and more exciting forms of solidarity in the quest for a world based on equality and social justice for all.

Deborah Eade
Editor, *Development in Practice*

February 1996

Notes

1 A phrase coined by Betsy Hartmann and James K. Boyce in *A Quiet Violence: View from a Bangladesh Village*, London: Zed Books (1993).

2 The 'apartheid of gender' was the central theme of the 1993 UNICEF annual report, *The State of the World's Children*, Oxford/New York: Oxford University Press.

3 UNDP: *Human Development Report 1995*, Oxford/New York: Oxford University Press.

Understanding difference and building solidarity:
a challenge to development initiatives

Mary B. Anderson

People — as individuals — differ, and peoples — as groups and societies — differ. Those of us who work within the framework of broad social movements, including the area(s) of international social and economic development, must acknowledge that such differences exist, even as we seek to apply encompassing solutions to large and comprehensive problems.

Development theory and practice of the 1950s and 1960s generally assumed that poverty was more or less homogeneous and that effective poverty alleviation efforts would, in a reasonable period of time, spread sufficiently to include most people. Experience showed these assumptions to be mistaken. Increasingly in the last thirty years, therefore, development analysts, policy-makers, and practitioners (very often responding to evidence brought forward by groups who found themselves excluded through development efforts) have identified categorisations of people who are 'left out' of generalised development processes and who, therefore, require special programming attention. Specifically, we have learned through practical experience, and through analysis of this experience, that certain groups — for example, women, the elderly, children, and others who are marginalised by their societies because of race, ethnicity, religion, or language — very often do not participate in or benefit from development programmes that are generally applied, even when these programmes are recognised as

'successful' in meeting their stated objectives. We have learned that awareness of the intrinsic socio-political structures that determine economic and social roles in any society is an essential ingredient of effective development programming.

The papers in this collection deal with a variety of categories of people and analyse the role assignments, both natural and socially-constructed, that make their circumstances of special concern for development practitioners. They raise and examine central issues of cultural blindness on the part of 'outsider' aid providers who fail to recognise the realities of 'insider' aid recipients.[1] And they propose helpful and important shifts in thinking and programming that are required if development assistance is to serve all of the people it is intended to serve. The advantages and fundamental necessity of recognising differences and diversity are amply demonstrated through these articles.

In this Introduction, however, I shall take a somewhat different approach. I shall argue that the current emphases in international development assistance on recognising differences and appreciating diversity have both positive and negative impacts. In the first section, I begin by examining the gains in development programming that are realised from recognising differences. In the second section, I turn to the corresponding examination of disadvantages that have arisen both for programming and for outcomes when development practitioners misapply the methodologies that highlight difference. In the third section, I pull the two together and discuss the importance of programming on the basis of differences — but of doing so in ways that unite, rather than distinguish, people's interests and that advocate shared societal progress, rather than only special (albeit justified) sub-group empowerment. I conclude that those of us who work internationally must find a way to maintain a balance between appreciation of difference and affirmation of sameness, between programming according to special circumstances and programming for commonality.

The 'good' of recognising differences and appreciating diversity

Recognition of differences

As noted above, early development assistance efforts failed to take account of differences within communities and, thereby, failed both to integrate and benefit all parts of society. The result of this failure was that some people gained from international assistance, while others were systematically excluded and disadvantaged. Foremost among groups that were excluded were women. In country after country, through project after project, the evidence mounted during the 1970s and 1980s that development assistance benefitted male members of societies at the expense of female members of societies.[2] Men gained access to technologies, while women did not; boys entered and completed schooling at rates that far exceeded those of girls; cash crops — largely in the domain of male farmers — were encouraged at the expense of food crops, which were the responsibility of women. Furthermore, evidence also emerged that the distribution of the gains realised through development assistance were not shared equally *within* families and households. Male family members were often fed before their

mothers, wives, daughters, and sisters; when family resources were scarce, parents chose to take sons to the clinic when they were ill, but waited, sometimes too long, to see if their daughters would get well without medical assistance; men who earned extra cash through wage labour or the sale of cash crops bought 'luxury' items such as radios and bicycles, while women, whose income sources were shrinking, remained responsible for household food, health, and education and, as they were pressured to meet increasing family needs with fewer resources, favoured sons over daughters, thereby reinforcing the cycle of advantage and disadvantage.

The importance of the recognition of these unintended but systematic consequences of economic change, often brought on and encouraged by external aid, cannot be overemphasised. So long as women, and their roles as producers and distributors in the economic sphere, were 'invisible' to aid planners, the damaging impacts of assistance on them — and, hence, on their families — continued. Many development projects failed because their designers and implementers did not recognise the relevance of gender analysis; as a result, scarce development resources have not produced the broad social and economic benefits that were intended. Attention to women and development, and the introduction of and refinements to Gender Analysis, have made a contribution to development theory and practice that should no longer be questioned by anyone with development experience.

As experience in analysing women's roles and circumstances grew, an appreciation of the importance of other differences also emerged. Development analysts and practitioners found that the assumption of homogeneity in any beneficiary population was a mistake which led to ineffective programming. In addition to acknowledging the differences of women's and men's roles and status, we found it useful to 'disaggregate' populations according to urban and rural contexts, by age groupings, and, often, according to sub-population groups defined by language, ethnicity, clan, religion, or race.

It is important to note that our motivation for identifying such groups was born, primarily, from negative experiences. We were alerted to the importance of differences, because we observed that programmes planned without attention to them did not reach everyone. The categories of people whom we identified were, in general, seen to be 'marginalised' or 'vulnerable'. We shall come back to this in the second section below.

The adoption of disaggregation methodologies[3] resulted in several distinct benefits in development programming.

First, these methodologies overcame the exceedingly important problem of 'invisibility'. That is, they alerted development practitioners to the fact that difference does exist, and it led them to analyse both why it exists and how its existence interacts with the implementation of development activities. Both the recognition of difference and the ensuing understanding of its place and dynamic within societies were essential elements of understanding the context where any effort was to be initiated.

Second, knowing that some groups were excluded from automatic inclusion in benefits allowed development assistance to be directed and honed, so that it reached those groups whose special needs were identified or who would, otherwise, have been left out.

Third, understanding how exclusion of some groups occurs allowed development practitioners to develop more intelligent and accurate strategies for overcoming disadvantage through development assistance. If disadvantage were 'natural' — that is, the inevitable result of innate characteristics of a certain group — then programmes might simply be developed to meet the needs of such groups as an act of charity. However, recognition that the systems which marginalise people according to a 'natural' characteristic such as sex, age, or race, are *socially* constructed meant that one could devise strategies for altering and reconstructing systems to end marginalisation.

Finally, recognition of difference and the systems that reinforce it allowed development

practitioners to set priorities among competing demands for scarce resources. From observing how existing systems lock certain people into disadvantaged positions, they could set priorities among various programme options in order to focus effort and resources on strategies that would most effectively address these systems and enable people to break out of the traps of impoverishment.

These advantages, gained through the recognition of difference, and its systemic creation and re-creation, are great. Development efforts (both international and indigenous) are remarkably improved when they apply the methodologies for disaggregation that have been developed in the past two decades.

Appreciation of diversity

Even as the development assistance community was learning to recognise and to programme in ways that incorporated differences, it was also moving towards an overdue and equally important appreciation of diversity. (The articles in this collection attest to both the importance and momentum of this movement.)

Again, in the 1950s and 1960s, international development assistance provided by countries of the North to countries of the South generally assumed a single development model, based on European and North American experience in the Industrial Revolution.[4] And, again, evidence of failed development efforts in many places revealed the inappropriateness of this assumption. Development practitioners came to see and appreciate the fact that cultures differ and that models of development must take account of diversity if they are to succeed.

Socio-cultural diversity — the rich variety of ways in which people and peoples assemble their systems of belief and values, of working and surviving, and of living in relationships with others — has thus assumed a central place in the thinking and planning of development workers. The appreciation of diversity forces abandonment of formulaic development approaches. Local contextual realities assume priority in the planning of development strategies and programmes.

Distinct advantages are also realised in development programming when diversity is recognised and appreciated.

The first advantage, again, is awareness. Past (and present!) failures of development programming often reflect a misfit between expectations and values imported from one context and the realities of the context where they were applied. To see and to appreciate as valid the existing realities and capacities of people whom development efforts are intended to assist is essential for accurate planning and programming.

Second, when providers of development assistance appreciate local realities and directly incorporate these into plans for developmental change, this ensures that local people, those actually doing the work of their own development, assume responsibility and ownership of their developmental directions and processes. This is essential for what is now referred to as 'sustainability'.

Third, and probably most important, when development practitioners (especially those who act as 'experts') truly appreciate socio-cultural diversity, they undertake their work (whether it is a long-term engagement or a short-term consultancy) on the basis of genuine respect for the people with whom they work. There is strong evidence that such respect on the part of the aid provider for the culture and capacities of the people is a major, if not the primary, determinant of whether people are motivated to engage in the activity of development and, thus, of whether the aid actually achieves its intended outcomes.

Clearly, the case is strong indeed that effective development programming must be based on a recognition of differences and an appreciation of diversity. Much good comes from both. Unfortunately, experience also shows that a misapplied emphasis on dis-aggregating population groups and on appreciating cultural diversity in order to focus programming efforts may have negative consequences, as well as positive ones.

Possible negative consequences of programming based on differences and diversity

Recognition of differences

As we noted above, attention to differences was initially motivated by recognition that certain groups were regularly disadvantaged by mainstream development. Thus, disaggregation methodologies are directed primarily towards identifying problem areas. That is, disaggregation is used to identify 'vulnerable' or 'marginalised' groups. What often occurs, then, is that development initiatives are undertaken only on the basis of needs and deprivations, and fail either to recognise or to build on the capacities of the groups to whom the aid is offered. The situation of women provides an example. As it has become commonplace to recognise that women are marginalised from economic and political power and that they are, thus, more vulnerable to poverty and crises than men, it has also become commonplace to assume that femaleness automatically equates with 'vulnerability'. While women are, indeed, more vulnerable to marginalisation and all of its attendant disadvantages than men, they also have immense strengths. They produce, they manage, they nurture, they maintain households and communities in the midst of hardship, and so on. While it is neither necessary nor inevitable that giving attention to differences and vulnerabilities will also result in ignoring capacities, experience shows that, too often, this does occur.

Second, among development agencies that recognise the importance of identifying differences as a way of focusing their programming there is a tendency to perceive and treat all vulnerable groups in the same way. We find, for example, repeated references to 'women and children', as if they comprise one group and as if their circumstances are the same. Of course it is true that women's concerns include, and hence overlap with, those of children. However, while children (at least very young ones) are dependent entirely on others in order to survive, women are not.

Putting women and children into one programming category obscures, again, the capacities of women, infantilises them, and results in poor programming. It would be similarly wrong to aggregate different minority groups, or people in other categories of disadvantage, without careful analysis.

Third, the categorisation of people may obscure important differences *within* a categorised group. To use the example of women again, all women are not the same. In some situations, the fact that women are rich or poor, urban or rural, educated or not may be a more important determinant of their circumstances — and, thus, of appropriate programme activities to support their development — than the fact that they are women *per se*.

Fourth, the reliance on categories of people as a way of focusing activities has led some development agencies to define their programmes as if the group with whom they are working is in a static and fixed position over time, rather than involved in dynamic and changing roles and relationships. For example, if an agency is committed to working with 'the poorest of the poor' and learns through gender analysis that women fall into this group, agency staff may (and have been seen to) fail to recognise changes that occur in women's circumstances. If programming were effective, women should move out of the category of 'poorest' and the agency should shift its focus to another group. Very often, designation of certain groups as the target of effort at one time will become inappropriate later but, because of the fixed categorisation of peoples, a development effort may continue to focus — wrongly — on the first-designated group.

Fifth, to call attention to disadvantage through attention to difference can, sometimes, result in misdirected programming. For example, while women may be marginalised from employment in a certain context, the most appropriate way to improve their access to work may be to focus not on the women themselves, but on some other aspect of the employment picture, such as legislation or transport or company incentives. Very often

when designating a particular disadvantaged group as needing change, development practitioners focus their efforts only on that group, rather than on other (possibly advantaged) groups who may hold the key to the required change.

It should be clear that none of these five possible negative consequences of differentiating among populations is either inevitable or necessary. They represent misuse or partial use of the tools for improving programmes through disaggregation.

However, each does occur, repeatedly, both in field operations and in decision-making at headquarters. To avoid misuse of the tools of disaggregation, development agencies need to be aware of these potential pitfalls and must develop their analytic capabilities to ensure dynamic and appropriate categorisation of people's differences in any context where they are working. Assumptions about differences carried from one locale to another can never be more than partially accurate. They must be reexamined and reevaluated over time, and from place to place.

Appreciating diversity

An emphasis on the importance of recognising and appreciating cultural diversity can also have negative consequences in development programming. Two possible pitfalls deserve discussion.

First, recognition of diversity sometimes leads to complete 'ad hocism'. If every place and every culture is different, then (some believe) we must empty our minds of past experiences as we approach each new area. The result is that there is no attention to cumulating and codifying lessons about effective programming.

The issue is not simple. We have just noted in the paragraphs above that assumptions about differences carried from one locale to another can be wrong. We now raise the danger that development practitioners will fail to learn from experience and fail to improve their effectiveness if they regard each programme-setting as different from all other locations.

How can one remain open to differences and, at the same time, learn from and accumulate experience, so that development efforts become increasingly effective?

One answer to this apparent conundrum lies in learning to ask the right questions as a basis for designing development programmes — questions which are common to all settings — rather than in applying a common solution which is unlikely to be appropriate from one place to the next. Disaggregation methodologies discussed in the previous section provide systems for asking such questions. From experience, we have learned that in *every* society there are some groups who are disadvantaged relative to other groups. Who, why, and in what way this occurs varies from society to society (according to socio-political and cultural diversity). From experience, we have learned how to ask questions that will help us to learn, in any society, how roles are assigned to different groups, how resources (both material and political) are divided, and what factors lie behind and shape these role-assignments and resource-divisions. Recognising that patterns differ from society to society, but using past experience to alert us to what to look for and how, allows us to abandon *assumptions* and to find out facts that are critical for effective programming. Thus, if disaggregation is rightly understood and diversity is well appreciated, it is not necessary to approach each situation with a blank mind and to develop *ad hoc* programming without benefit of past experience.

The second dilemma raised by emphasising the importance of appreciating cultural diversity is more difficult. This is the tendency for an appreciation of differences to be translated into total cultural relativism. Some people feel that an appreciation of local customs and values entails suspension of judgement about them. Everything that exists in a society is accepted as valid for that society and, therefore, not to be tampered with by outside aid providers. Very often, however, appreciation of cultural diversity is used to justify the acceptance of systems of dominance and exploitation that exist within societies. A primary example of this is the claim made by some international and indigenous development practitioners that assistance should not undertake to change the relationships between men and women in the societies where it is offered. Again, the issue is not simple. What is an appropriate balance between a commitment to universal values (such as equality) and an appreciation of local values that differ from (or deny) the universal values to which one is committed?

Answers to this apparent conundrum are offered in several of the papers included in this volume. Decisions of agencies and individuals about where and how to express disagreement with local values always reflect both the depth of disagreement and the realities of any given context. In my experience, however, an 'outsider' is never in the position of, alone, representing some 'universal' value. Rather, within every society, there are individuals and groups who are themselves engaged in propagation of the values considered 'universal'. Moreover, aid workers' claims that appreciation of local culture forces silence in areas where 'outsiders' disagree are disingenuous, in that the very act of working for development amounts to a declaration that all is not right with the situation prevailing in the area of work. All development and humanitarian assistance interacts and interferes with local structures and systems and, if effective, reinforces changes in these structures and systems that some parts of the local society seek and other parts, very likely, resist. To pretend otherwise is to deny the very purpose of the effort. Explicit acknowledgment of areas of disagreement, coupled with understanding of local culture and respect for the people but not for the specific values with which one disagrees, provides a basis for continuing dialogue and exploration of differences. I would argue that honesty about differences in values is an essential element of respect; to remain silent about areas where there are differences of values is to show disrespect for the other's ability to join in debate and the mutual search for common ground.

We have explored difficulties and problems that arise both from misapplied recognition of differences and from too facile an emphasis on appreciation of cultural diversity, and we have suggested some possible ways of addressing these difficulties. Though I have explored these possible negative outcomes, readers should be in no doubt about this author's commitment to both disaggregation methodologies and the appreciation of diversity as essential elements of effective development and humanitarian assistance. International (and insider) assistance cannot be well offered without these elements, and it is for this reason that we must be alert to their wrong application as well.

This stated, we turn now to a seemingly new (but perhaps quite old) challenge that development practitioners face as they seek to navigate through the shoals of difference and diversity. If there were a chance that my discussion, above, of possible difficulties could be misinterpreted as an excuse for not doing gender analysis or, otherwise, programming with attention to differences, then the dangers of misinterpretation of what follows are even greater. I caution and implore readers to be attentive to the dilemmas I am attempting to raise for our further, collective exploration, as I am convinced from my own experience that, if we fail to face the difficulties I will discuss below (as well as above), we shall risk doing more harm than good with the people whom we seek to help.

When differences lead to widespread violent conflict

Over the years, narrow attention to improving income levels has been replaced by broad attention to social, political, and cultural elements in development programming. Attempts to understand how people are excluded from sharing in their societies' wealth motivated not only recognition of differences and diversity, as noted above, but also explicit programming efforts to overcome that exclusion. Thus, many development efforts have focused on alleviating poverty and have, as a result, operated in alliance with the poor. Non-governmental organisations in particular have taken up development efforts as an

expression of their commitment to justice and against exploitation. They have used the mechanism of development programming to express 'solidarity' with those whom they see as suffering from unjust systems. Their commitment to justice has demanded that they 'side with' those who suffer injustice.

In taking on the just cause of the poor, development programming has often promoted confrontation between those it is intended to help and those seen as perpetuating unjust systems. Development practitioners speak of 'empowering' those without power; they organise and encourage women's (and other) groups to analyse the causes of their oppression and to recognise their power to affect change.

This is good. Injustice must be confronted and power should be shared. However, the outbreak of multiple, civilian-based wars within societies since the end of the Cold War has caused me to take another look at the impacts of the well-intended alliances with the marginalised that we, in the development field, have pursued. A reexamination of our approaches of recent years shows that, very often, we have promulgated a perception that the evil which people experience in poverty, exclusion, etc. is embodied in some other group which holds wealth, power, etc. We have identified 'problems' with people, and we have encouraged those with whom we work also to do so.

This approach entails problems. Let me suggest three.

First, as we noted in the previous section, it is wrong to assume homogeneity in any group of people whom we identify as needing our support. It is equally wrong to assume that 'oppressor' groups are homogeneous. Within all privileged groups there are individuals who, though they benefit from existing systems, are extremely uncomfortable with these systems. They often take immense risks and sometimes sacrifice their lives and livelihoods to end their own privilege. In addition, there are always people who benefit, without thought, from socio-political systems and who are threatened by the idea of change through which (they fear) they will not only lose their privilege but also be dominated by some other group. However, these are not evil people. If approached with a vision of how change might result in benefits for all, many of these individuals can be enlisted in the pursuit of broadened justice. Both the sacrificial few and the not-selfish many could become allies for social and political change, if they were allowed to do so; but categorisations of people as 'those in power' have too often limited our ability to differentiate among them and to see them as worthy of association and common planning.

Second, a programmatic emphasis on differences and diversity has, in some cases, supported tendencies towards social disintegration and divisiveness. In the power vacuums that followed the end of the Cold War, opportunistic leaders emerged in a number of places who found that their power could be consolidated through manipulation of sub-group identities. Too often, these leaders defined their societies' problems in inter-group terms and encouraged their followers to define their own access to justice and power in opposition to the attainment of these by other groups. In too many cases, these so-called leaders have excited people to conflict on the basis of these identities, citing past wrongs and injustices as the motivator of their warfare. But in country after country (current Afghanistan, former Yugoslavia, southern Tajikistan, Somalia ... the list can be extended),[5] the evidence is strong that such 'leaders' are really only pursuing power and, by the techniques they rely on, perpetuating inter-group injustice, rather than creating systems for ensuring broadly inclusive justice.

Has international assistance caused such conflicts? The answer is clearly 'no'. But it is also clear that, in many places where wars have recently broken out, these conflicts have not been started by poor or marginalised people in a 'people's revolution' (though these are the people most often enlisted into the fighting forces, because there are few other employment opportunities in their societies). Though disadvantage and injustice are often cited as the 'root causes' of war, the evidence is strong that civil wars in which former neighbours, co-workers, and, even, family members take up arms against each other do little to further either equality or justice. And, sadly, there is some evidence that the promotion of differences by the international aid community can be put to the use of and reinforce social divisiveness where it exists.

Finally, one should ask, if we seek to identify sub-groupings of society that have been silenced through amalgamation into the whole, where might this ultimately end? Will the groups that deserve external support for recognition of their rights get smaller and smaller? Will identities be formed around more and more special and particular histories? If so, how will societies accommodate the centrifugal forces of such sub-group splits?[6]

Towards a balance of difference and sameness

We began this essay by noting that people and peoples differ. We end by noting that people and peoples have much in common. While important differences exist in experience, in access, in status, and in roles, it is also true that important samenesses prevail across human experience, struggles, and activities. If both are true, how might the development community maintain its commitment to recognising differences because they are central for effective programme design and, at the same time, initiate programmes that encourage recognition of common interests and shared values? If, after all, people need to live together in this world, what strategies may we discover by which to overcome injustice without, at the same time, increasing inter-group hostilities and creating anew the systems of dominance and oppression in which the actors only trade places, but the actions continue?

As he led the movement for Independence from Britain in India, Mohandas Gandhi always instructed his followers to differentiate between oppression and oppressors. He enjoined people to fight with all their strength against oppression, but to work with the oppressor to change the systems that entrapped them both. Of course, not all oppressors want to be worked 'with' to end their dominance. But the point is still salient. Again, I ask the reader not to misunderstand my point. As Gandhi said, oppression must be resisted and overcome. The issue I am raising here is an issue of approach, of strategy. How might we best engage in the pursuit of justice to ensure that we do not create or reinforce other injustices along the way? Given past experience and especially recent experience, we should challenge ourselves to greater levels of creativity and exploration.

We must find ways to promote economic and social well-being for those who have been left out — ways that also appeal to the humanity of those who have benefitted from existing systems. We must develop programming approaches, and systems of economy and society, that acknowledge differences and diversity and, at the same time, unite rather than distinguish people's interests. We must work to empower marginalised groups — not in relation to other people, but in relation to their participation in decisions and actions that affect their lives. We are on the steep rise of a learning curve about the impacts — intended and unintended — of development assistance. As we develop tools of analysis that help us to see who is disadvantaged and how disadvantage occurs, we must also develop new tools of action that undo these systems without pitting people, and groups of people, against each other.

December 1995

Notes

1 I use quotation marks to designate 'insiders' and 'outsiders', in order to reflect the fact that, very often, aid workers from inside the country where aid is given are perceived as, and exhibit qualities of, outsiders. Their experiences and attitudes (often urban or educated) may be as 'foreign' as those from other lands and cultures, and may just as surely distance them from the intended beneficiaries of their aid. In this paper, I am referring primarily to issues which are pertinent to international assistance, because I, myself, belong to the 'international aid body'. However, much if not most of what is said applies, I believe, also to indigenous NGO and other local aid efforts.

2 C. Overholt, M. B. Anderson, K. Cloud and J.E. Austin (eds): *Gender Roles in Development Projects: A Case Book* (Kumarian Press, West Hartford, CN, 1995).

3 Such methodologies include Gender Analysis, Rapid Rural Appraisal Techniques, Capacities and Vulnerabilities Analysis, People-Oriented Planning, and others. The point of each of these approaches is to help aid workers to identify those characteristics of people in any community to be aided that matter the most in terms of affecting the design and implementation of aid efforts.

4 Some might argue that there were two exported development models: that of Western capitalism and that of Soviet socialism. My own analysis is that these two approaches reflect the same set of assumptions. While one sees capital as primary in motivating growth, and the other places labour at the centre of wealth, both were developed in the context of, and in response to, the Industrial Revolution of Europe, and they use the same units of analysis (viz. land, labour, and capital).

5 I have personally been told this by people from the countries named, as well as Sri Lanka, India, and Lebanon.

6 Ethiopia is a case in point. Whereas this country has been known for centuries as a multi-tribal entity, the current policy of designating particular areas for specific subgroups and emphasising and honouring language differences leads some close observers (including Ethiopians) to wonder whether this will end by promoting fragmentation rather than mutual appreciation and fairness. Similarly, I have been told by Sri Lankans that one major mistake made in that country was the decision to drop a common language requirement in schools, so that now few Sinhalese and Tamils who wish to do so have the ability to communicate with each other.

Gender, development, and training:
raising awareness in the planning process

Naila Kabeer

Introduction

In an important paper analysing how poor people have been marginalised in development efforts, Robert Chambers (1983) identifies some of the biased procedures of researchers and practitioners during their visits to the countryside. These include *seasonal bias* (visiting during the dry, cool, and often less hungry times of year); *people bias* (meeting only the more influential members of a village); and *roadside bias* (visiting only villages which are conveniently located by the tarmac road, and missing poorer villages in the interior). Of course, these biases are not simply accidents or mistakes: they also reflect the social and conceptual distance between those who plan and the disempowered sections among those planned for.

More than a decade of research on the problematic status of women in development has helped to uncover the many biases that work to keep women marginal in the development process. Some of this work points to gender biases in assumptions and procedures, equivalent to the poverty biases identified by Chambers. Others question the validity of dominant notions of development. This article[1] sketches out some aspects of the former, in order to give substance to the challenge of the latter. It represents the underlying rationale for our training efforts in gender and development at the Institute of Development Studies (IDS) at the University of Sussex, where we run courses of varying duration for development practitioners and researchers from different parts of the world.[2] These courses offer participants the opportunity to examine the ways in which women have been included and excluded in past development efforts, and the chance to develop new and more equitable frameworks for thinking about gender and development.

Keeping women out: lessons from development practice

In the true 'hunter-gatherer' manner of trainers, I have made use of an extremely helpful checklist compiled by Marilyn Waring for the Women and Development section of UNDP, in which she has summarised some of the well-tried and tested ways of keeping women invisible in development planning — the gender equivalent of Chambers' poverty biases.[3] She covers both well-known, more blatant procedures (for example, insisting on male project officers who can be relied on to 'mightily under-report' women's activities), as well as other lesser-known and more subtle techniques.

I find Waring's list an excellent training tool for three reasons. First, because it brings together in a succinct fashion the critiques made by a number of specialists in this field. Second, because by expressing her list in the negative — purportedly as a guide to those planners (presumably, but not necessarily male) who continue to believe that development is by, for, and about men, it offers a humorous and thought-provoking route into discussion about these critical issues. Third, because it provokes development practitioners in different cultural contexts to compile their own local versions of the ways in which planners have ensured that men are the primary beneficiaries of the development budget. What follows is a free and personal interpretation of some of Waring's tips (she will be cited specifically when these are used), together with a few I have added from my own observations.

Things, not people

Concentrate on things, rather than people. Concentrate on getting roads, bridges, and buildings built, and argue that it is up to someone else (the social adviser; the women's ministry; the Women in Development (WID) unit; the welfare sector; the token woman in the organisation) to take care of the human and social implications. Alternatively you might argue that:

• Since you have not mentioned either men or women in your project plan, your project is gender-neutral.

• That though you mention only men as beneficiaries, you are using the term to include women.

• Or, finally, that 'women-walk-on-roads-too'. This category of justification was the creative invention of a field mission of the US Agency for International Development, which included a road construction project as a WID activity on the basis that 'women walk on roads too' (cited in Maguire, 1984).

Fallacies of aggregation

If you have to plan for people as well as things, Waring's advice is: 'Always use non-specific or generic categories such as labour force, producers, consumers, holder, head of household, reference person, poor, homeless, malnutritive, illiterate, unemployed'. One might add that if you are a radical, you might prefer terms such as 'the people', 'the peasants', 'the community', 'the workers', 'the masses', 'the proletariat', or 'the reserve army of labour'. The main thing is not to get bogged down by details such as age or gender. This way you can maintain the illusion that you are dealing with a harmonious and internally undifferentiated category of people, all of whose members have the same needs and will be served equally well by the same set of projects; then you won't have to deal with the vexatious issues of conflict and power.

These abstract and aggregative concepts are, of course, frequently linguistic disguises for conceptual inadequacies. In reality, the poor, the community, the labour force, etc. are internally differentiated categories of people, unified only by definitional fiat. Let me illustrate this point by discussing three particular variants of this 'fallacy of aggregation', and demonstrate how they help to render women invisible.

'The poor'

Here the convention might be stated as: treat 'the poor' as that anonymous mass of people who fall below an arbitrarily designated threshold called 'the poverty line'. You need know nothing further about them. Rely instead on your preconceptions to design poverty-alleviation strategies. Most popular are public works programmes for men and handicraft schemes for women; the difference between them is that one is believed to generate employment, while the other generates only income.

The conventional way of conceptualising and measuring poverty has relied heavily on household income as the main indicator in calculating the poverty line. However, this will be an accurate measure only if all household members have equal claim on household income and are therefore equally poor. Alternative measurements which do not rely solely on household income, but conceptualise poverty in the broader sense of deprivation and vulnerability, and which measure the distribution of poverty *within* communities and households, strongly point to gender as a factor in explaining individual welfare differentials (Kabeer 1991).

The simple insight behind this is that ultimately it is not households or communities which are poor, but individual women, men, and children. Losing sight of the distribution of poverty among individuals carries the danger of ignoring the disproportionate presence of certain categories (particularly women and young children) in the ranks of the deprived and disenfranchised sections of the community.

'The household'

Here the convention has been: treat the household as a homogeneous and harmonious group of people. Then you can argue that the head of household is the principal decision-making authority in the household; you need to consult only with him, since he has the best interests of other members at heart. You notice I refer to the head as 'he'; you must take this for granted: it will save you a lot of time and trouble later. You can even treat a male member who is generally absent from the household as its head, as this will protect you from any need to consult female household members.

This variant of the 'fallacy of aggregation' has been much criticised, but is alive and thriving. A major household survey carried out by the World Bank in the 1980s in a number of African countries — the Living Standards Measurement Survey — offers limited information on intra-household gender dimensions, precisely because of this kind of assumption. And it is still common to find planners taking it for granted that once the benefits of development 'trickle down' to the head of the household (i.e. any adult male), they will then 'trickle across' to other members of the household. Little notice is taken of the well-authenticated research findings from a number of countries that egalitarianism is not a necessary feature of households.

In South Asia, there are data to show that women and children, especially young girls, are likely to be discriminated against in the distribution of food and other life-preserving resources (Sen 1990). From sub-Saharan Africa there is evidence that children are often nutritionally better-off in households where women have control over income or crops (Longhurst 1988). Finally, research in the UK shows that many women report being financially better off after leaving their husbands, despite the fact that they have to survive on state welfare (Pahl, 1984). The gist of these findings is that, in both First and Third World contexts, men frequently keep a disproportionate amount of their incomes for their own use, depriving their wives and children of badly needed resources. Addressing power relations within the family is not about destroying the family, as some have alleged, but about seeking to transform it into a more equitable institution.

'Women'

If you are pressured by some misguided do-gooder in your ministry or organisation into agreeing to take women into account in your projects, then simply assume that (since you yourself personally know many women) you know what their needs are likely to be.

The absurdity of the assumption that you can devise programmes for a social category labelled 'women' becomes clear when you consider that few project planners would dream of devising projects for an undifferentiated category labelled 'men'. Women (as academics are fond of saying) are not a homogeneous group. They are differentiated by class, religion, culture, age, and life-cycle, so that in any given context, their needs have to be investigated rather than assumed.

Yet project after project has been devised for poor and assetless women in Asia and Africa which has sought to teach them skills — baking, sewing, knitting, home economics — which are totally inappropriate to their economic needs, but do conform to particular planners' views about appropriate feminine occupations. Of course, acting on such preconceptions about women's needs has the added advantage that it saves planners the time and effort that might otherwise be spent on finding out about the actual needs of actual women.

In a Bangladeshi NGO I once visited, its staff complained that it was useless offering free literacy classes for poor women, since they refused to attend. Closer examination revealed that literacy classes were held at a time of day when most landless women were earning their livelihoods in domestic and post-harvest labour for the wealthy. The NGO was operating with an implicit assumption that the opportunity cost of women's time was zero, and yet they appeared to be irrationally rejecting a free good. In a different context, a government official from Ghana at a recent training course at IDS complained that he found it was useless trying to involve women in his projects, because they seemed to prefer spending all their time in market trading. In both cases, it appeared that women were being planned for, but with little consultation or indeed knowledge about their own perceived needs and priorities.

If it can't be counted, it doesn't count

If you have to turn to empirical information in your planning efforts, protect your ignorance about women's lives by careful selection of the kind of data you consult. Waring's tip here is brief and to the point: 'Use national census data whenever possible (on the grounds that other data collection is too expensive or "conceptually difficult". This way you will be able to engage in all kinds of creative omissions, inclusions and definitions.' As she points out, you will usually be able to omit 'unpaid family workers, seasonal workers, subsistence production ... home-based crop processing ... all labour by children under the age of 15 and all the labour, production and consumption undertaken by the woman called a housewife'. Moreover, you will be able to call men and women's agricultural activities by different names — farming (men's activities) and kitchen gardening (women's activities) or use the simpler distinction of 'working' and 'helping' — thereby bestowing them with unequal value in the national accounts.

There are other forms of census practice that have ensured that women's productive contributions are effectively underplayed:

• Asking only about 'primary' occupation. Most women are likely to state 'housework' as their primary occupation, but the term carries very different implications for urban and rural areas, and for the wealthy and the poor. Housework in the countryside is more likely to include a variety of agricultural tasks (post-harvest processing and storage; fuel and water collection; livestock and poultry care, etc.), and housework among the poor more likely to contain a greater variety of income-stretching activities, rather than management and supervisory functions. A classic example of bad census practice comes from India, where the priority given to 'primary occupation' in the 1971 census, compared with the 1961 census, partly accounted for the drastic decline of 28 million recorded for rural women workers.

• Asking only about 'current' rather than 'usual' work status. This way, given the greater multiplicity of domestic and agricultural tasks that women engage in, the census is more likely to omit women who at the time of data collection are engaged in domestic tasks. The twenty-seventh round of the National Sample Survey in India found little difference between the two definitions as far as participation in the rural male labour force and participation in the urban male and female labour forces were concerned. However, it netted in an additional 6 million rural women under the 'usual status' definition, compared with the 'current status' one.

• Another form of bias is pointed out by Renée Pittin for the 1952 Nigerian census, which allowed for six categories of work for men and only three for women, of which one category was 'other' (1987). In one district, Pittin notes that 90 per cent of women fell into the category of 'other', and planners were none the wiser about what it was that women did. Not surprisingly, the Department of Statistics was led to the conclusion that 'The three occupational groups for females have not provided as useful an indication of primary occupations as the male groups' (cited in Pittin 1987: 32).

• Finally, all activities whose products do not enter extensively into the market are omitted from GNP accounts since they cannot be given a monetary value. Consequently, the labour of child-bearing, child care, and care of the ill, the disabled, and elderly members of the family are all rendered invisible. As N.S. Jodha has pointed out, there is a very thin line indeed between not counting in an activity in project planning because you cannot measure it and then either denying that it exists, or seeing it as valueless and therefore a minus in GNP accounts, a drain on the national wealth.

All these procedures of naming, counting, omitting, and including have very practical implications, since they determine how resources are to be allocated by planners. If an activity is not considered to contribute to the GNP, then any allocation of resources to it appears to be on the grounds of welfare rather than efficiency, somehow second-best and first to be dispensed with in times of economic scarcity.

Sectoral planning for inter-sectoral realities

Neatly dovetailing with my last point is Waring's next piece of advice: 'Adopt a sectoral approach to development in general, and to each project in particular'. This has two important advantages. First of all, you can divide your sectors into those with efficiency implications (agriculture, industry, finance, and foreign trade) and those with welfare implications (health, family planning, poverty alleviation, women, and children). This immediately gives you a hierarchy of priorities, with efficiency-related projects having first claim as *economic assets* (otherwise, as you argue, there would be no resources), and welfare-related projects mopping up residual resources as *economic liabilities*.

Secondly, sectoral planning helps you to sidestep the problem of considering inter-sectoral implications. By ignoring them, you make sure they become someone else's problem. In fact, they are most likely to become women's problem. Piecemeal and compart-mentalised planning has allowed different

groups of planners to focus narrowly on single aspects of people's lives and to plan their projects with respect to that aspect alone. However, given the multiplicity of tasks that women, particularly poor women, have to perform in caring for their families and contributing to their livelihoods, the result is that they are subjected to a battery of contradictory signals from development initiatives.

Early development efforts focused on women as wives and mothers. This led to a proliferation of projects which sought to give them training in home economics and domestic skills, nutritional education, and family planning motivation. After much criticism of 'welfarist' approaches to women, there has been a recent shift to seeing women as economic agents and to targeting them for agricultural projects, export-oriented factories, and micro-enterprises. Much of the burden of so-called community health care falls on the main health carers at family level, again women. Using the aggregated concept of the community often disguises the fact that it is women who will be required to respond to primary health care messages. If this was more openly acknowledged, the delivery of health care services could be designed to suit women's existing work burdens and working schedule. More recently, with the new green agenda, there are proposals in the international forums for 'primary environmental care' projects, with the great danger that women as preservers of nature — as has been argued by some — will have yet another set of responsibilities to cope with.

The problem is that all of these assumptions are generally and simultaneously true. Women, particularly in poor Third World countries, are primarily responsible for child care and looking after the sick, disabled, and elderly; they are also producers of economic and financial resources for their families. In their roles as gatherers of wood and carriers of water, they have suffered from the commercial over-exploitation of natural resources and they have demonstrated innovation and creativity in their responses. Not surprisingly, available data on time allocation show that women work much longer hours than men almost everywhere in the world. The seamless web of women's lives, encompassing a variety of productive and reproductive activities, is easily discounted within piecemeal and sectoral planning processes.

This lack of fit between the sectoral thinking of planners and the inter-sectoral spread of women's activities is partly responsible for the failures of many projects which claimed to address women's needs. Projects designed in one sector targeting women take little account of whom other sectors might be targeting. Primary health-care projects, income-generating activities, public works poverty-alleviation programmes, and environmental projects are all set up, implicitly or explicitly targeting the same category of the population to participate in them. The result is conflicting demands on women's time, intensified work burdens and, in the longer run, project failures. And when a project fails, planners blame it not on their own myopic assumptions, but on the hopelessness of planning for women.

Needs and needs

Finally, if for some reason you have to demonstrate your gender awareness, incorporate women's needs into planning objectives, but use a selective definition of these needs. The point is that there are needs and needs, some arising out of the day-to-day reality of women's lives, and others arising out of the goal of transforming an inequitable reality (Molyneux 1985). Even in a situation where women have been identified as important to the development effort, *real* change can be resisted by selectively focusing on their practical needs, i.e. those requirements which help them to fulfil their roles and responsibilities, as defined by the existing gender-bound division of labour. These may be related to their roles as mothers, as family health carers, or even as productive agents, but they are needs which arise from how women are defined within the gender-determined *status quo*.

It is much easier to think of power as a feature of race, caste, and class relations than as a feature of relations between women and men, particularly those from the same family. As Waring points out, this leads to the widespread assumption that 'the family is the place where women and children find their material existence guaranteed and their physical safety secure'. Yet growing documentation, not just of the discrimination we noted above, but also of the violence against women — wife battering, rape, child abuse, and enforced child-bearing — suggests that not only is power a widespread feature of gender relations, but that it often takes a very coercive form.

Even when planners are aware of these aspects of women's subordination, they find it politically safer and more expedient to focus on those needs which will not threaten men's power and privileges. They prefer to overlook the strategic interests of women which arise out of their subordinate position in society and would require a radical transformation of interpersonal relations between women and men so that women have greater power over their own lives and men have less power over women's lives. They have successfully resisted learning from increasing numbers of non-governmental or political organisations which have made women's empowerment and men's conscientisation their primary objectives. Yet unless these strategic advances are made, even women's practical gains are likely to be reversed when resources dry up. This was observable during the 1980s as the international economic crisis forced many Third World governments to cut back on health, education and public sector employment.

Concepts for gender training for development planners

Highlighting the ways in which women have been kept out of development is a useful starting point for raising awareness about gender. However, gender training has to go beyond critiques of past project failures and beyond providing practitioners with check lists and guidelines within which to monitor their own performance. It must be about uncovering all those hidden and taken-for-granted ideas about gender that are brought into play in development planning. This section of the article provides some of the basic elements of an alternative approach to development: development with a gender perspective.

I began with Chambers' list of planning practices which contain a bias against the poor. He attributes these biased procedures to the values and preferences of development professionals, their distance from the poor, and the inadequate modes of learning in which they have been educated. In many ways, the gender biases we have mentioned are more difficult to identify and acknowledge, because they are concealed by deep-rooted ideologies about what is 'natural' and 'given'. There are of course 'naturalising' explanations of poverty (the poor are inferior, have lower IQs, etc.), but they have ceased to be accepted as legitimate explanations, except among the very bigoted. Yet differences and inequalities between the genders continue to be thought of as stemming from natural and biologically given differences between the sexes. These ideologies are something we have all grown up with, they are part of the prevailing 'common sense' in many cultures, and we all have a stake in their maintenance because they have taken deep roots in our identities. To challenge, or merely question, the prevailing divisions between women and men can in some sense also challenge one's sense of selfhood.

The aim of gender training is therefore to distinguish between what is natural and biological and what is culturally constructed, and in the process to renegotiate the boundaries between the natural — and hence apparently inflexible — and the social — and hence relatively transformable. The first component of our framework is therefore the distinction between 'biological' sex and 'socially constructed' gender; the distinction between the existence of sexual attributes and their cultural interpretations. Gender is seen as the process by which individuals who are born into biological categories of 'male' or 'female' become the social categories of men and women through the acquisition of locally-defined attributes of masculinity and femininity. While the process of acquiring gender identities — becoming men and women — may appear far removed from the concerns of development policy-makers and practitioners, it is in fact a critical starting point. It challenges the notion that men and women are somehow naturally suited to certain tasks or roles, and it starts to delineate those aspects of social reality which can be changed because they are not biologically given.

Moreover, understanding how deeply rooted are these ideological assumptions in our consciousness will help us to understand and anticipate the hostility of some women and many men, and their resistance to attempts to transform gender relations. Their opposition has included (a) appeals to culture and tradition — as though culture and tradition were somehow frozen for all time, rather than in a constant process of change; (b) accusations of Western cultural imperialism — as though Third World women were somehow incapable of making an autonomous analysis of their own situations; (c) the fears that acknowledgement of power relations within the family puts the entire institution in danger — rather than being a step towards greater egalitarianism; (d) and of course contemptuous 'humour' and outright hostility.

The second component of our gender and development framework is to examine and analyse the different relations and processes which construct gender in different cultures. A key reason for treating gender difference as socially constructed rather than naturally given is the cross-cultural diversity of its manifestations. One of the mistakes of development planning has been to assume that gender differences are biologically determined and therefore uniform in all contexts. Planners have therefore been guilty of operating with class-specific, urban-biased, ethnocentric models of gender relations, on the assumption that the model they were most familiar with was the sole possible model.

A relational approach to gender helps to dispel these misconceptions. It examines the key social relationships which produce the division of gender attributes, tasks, responsibilities, skills, and resources between women and men (see Whitehead 1979). The domain of family and kinship is a primary site for the construction of gender relations. Clearly marriage is an important example of such a relationship, but all relationships which structure interactions between and among the genders (brother, sister, mother, father, mother-in-law) are implicated in the social construction of gender identities and gender categories. While the relationships in which men and women interact outside the familial domain may not be intrinsically gendered, they become vehicles of the gendering process, because they reproduce gender differences in the positions of women and men. Women and men enter markets, political organisations, bureaucracies, and NGOs bearing the traits, skills, resources, capabilities, and aptitudes assigned to them on the basis of their gender; their experience within these institutions is likely to reflect and reproduce these divisions.

The third component of our framework is to focus in greater detail on a critical aspect of gender relations, the division of labour, which does not simply determine who does what tasks, but also how tasks will be valued, how skills and aptitudes are assigned to and acquired by women and men, and the distribution of socially valued resources which results from this division. The objectives are, first of all, to make visible the inter-linkages and synergies between the tasks associated with production and reproduction and those who carry them out; and secondly to point to the way in which different divisions of labour create different relations of interdependence and exchange between men and women. The first step for any form of development planning is to build up information on locally prevailing divisions of labour and the relationships of authority and control, on decision-making at different stages of the production process, and on the distribution of fruits of labour embodied in different patterns of labour relations.

The fourth component is to rethink the meaning of production in the light of our analysis of the gender-linked division of labour. We need to move away from definitions which privilege production for the market as a key criterion, or even production of material resources alone. A new perspective becomes possible if we step back to examine the goals of development. There is an emerging consensus that development requires enhancement of the human welfare and well-being of *all* members of society, regardless of age, gender, caste, etc. UNICEF's *Adjustment with a Human Face* (1987), the UNDP's *Human Development Report* (brought out for the first time in 1990), and the Commonwealth Secretariat's *Engendering Adjustment for the 1990s* (1989), and the World Bank's 1990 World Development Report *Poverty* are all evidence of these concerns.

From the point of view of our conceptual framework, the human factor is a critical starting point for all development planning, since human labour and creativity are inputs into the development process, and human well-being is the intended outcome. Activities which contribute to the everyday needs and generational reproduction of human beings and to their health and welfare should be seen as productive activities to be counted as assets in the national balance sheet, regardless of whether they are carried out through family, market, or bureaucratic agents. Such recognition will ensure that planners take account of these activities, and their inter-linkages, in allocating their priorities and resources. Expenditure on public provision of health and maternal and child care services will be seen not as unproductive forms of expenditure, but as productive investments in the nation's human capital and the key precondition to release female labour for other forms of productive activity. As Elson points out, expenditures on welfare services then become complementary to, rather than competitive with, efficiency considerations (1991).

Our fifth component shifts the focus from what *is* to what *could be*, from planning for practical needs to strategies for empowerment. While we do not offer blueprints for action — and do not believe that such blueprints are useful in this context — there are several different ways of analysing the issue of power as it relates to gender. What is most striking about the power dimension in gender relations is the extent to which ideologies about gender difference and gender inequalities are internalised as a natural state of affairs by women as much as by men. Empowering women must begin with the individual consciousness and with the imaginative construction of alternative ways of being, living, and relating. However, to bring about social change, it must move from changing our personal ways of thinking and doing to changing external realities; and here the lessons, victories, and setbacks of women's experiences in organising for their practical needs as well as their strategic interests become the raw material from which new strategies can be devised.

To conclude, our aim must be to get away from the abstract and aggregated concepts of development that planners have worked with in the past, and to work towards a more holistic understanding of it. This requires an awareness of the human and gender-linked implications of all forms of policy intervention, which is informed by the multiple interlinkages between production and reproduction, between the creation of material resources as well as human resources; which gives as much weight to process — *how* things get done — as to outcome — *what* gets done; and, finally, one which recognises that gender equity in social transformation requires the empowerment of women and alliances with men if it is to be a sustainable achievement. This is an ambitious project, because such social transformation must operate on the intersecting and dynamic sets of relationships which make up all our social realities. At the same time, for those who feel overwhelmed by the enormity of the task of challenging the boundaries of what is considered natural and hence beyond our power to change, we can cite Paulo Freire (cited in Maguire 1984) in saying:

Society now reveals itself as something unfinished, not as something inexorably given. It has become a challenge rather than a hopeless situation.

Notes

1 This article is based on a paper presented to the National Labour Institute/Ford Foundation Workshop on Gender Training and Development, Bangalore, December 1990.

2 While shorter courses are tailored to the needs of different constituencies, the main gender training at IDS takes place on a three-month short course entitled 'Women, Men and Development', run every 15 months at the Institute, and a one-year MA course in Gender and Development, which is co-directed with the University of Sussex.

3 Marilyn Waring was a Member of Parliament in New Zealand. She now works at writing and goat-farming. She has recently published a brilliant and witty dissection of the United Nations System of National Accounts in her book *If Women Counted* (Basingstoke: Macmillan, 1989).

References

Chambers, R., 1983, *Rural Development: Putting the Last First*, Harlow: Longman.

Elson, D., 1991, 'Male bias in macroeconomics: the case of structural adjustment' in D. Elson (ed), *Male Bias in the Development Process*, Manchester: Manchester University Press.

Kabeer, N., 1991, 'Gender dimensions of rural poverty: analysis from Bangladesh', *Journal of Peasant Studies*, 18/2.

Longhurst, R., 1988, 'Cash crops, household food security and nutrition', *IDS Bulletin*, 19/2.

Maguire, P., 1984, *Women in Development: An Alternative Analysis*, University of Massachusetts: Centre for International Education.

Molyneux, M., 1985, 'Mobilisation without emancipation? Women's interests, state and revolution in Nicaragua', *Feminist Studies*, 11/2.

Pahl, J., 1984, 'The allocation of money within the household' in M. Freeman (ed.): *The State, The Law, and the Family*, London: Tavistock Press.

Pittin, R., 1987, 'Documentation of women's work in Nigeria: problems and solutions' in C. Oppong (ed), *Sex Roles, Population and Development in West Africa*, London: James Currey, and New Hampshire: Heinemann Educational Books.

Sen, Amartya, 1990, 'Gender and co-operative conflict', in I. Tinker (ed.), *Persistent Inequalities*, Oxford: Oxford University ress.

Whitehead, A., 1979, 'Some preliminary notes on the subordination of women, *IDS Bulletin*, 10/3.

The author

Naila Kabeer has been a Fellow at the Institute of Development Studies at the University of Sussex since 1985, where she directs the course 'Women, Men and Development'. She is an economist working on gender and development, with a special interest in household economics, poverty, population, and health policies. She is a member of the Feminist Review Collective and on the Board of Directors of the PANOS Institute.

This article first appeared in *Development in Practice*, Volume 1, Number, in 1991.

Working with street children

Tom Scanlon, Francesca Scanlon, and Maria Luiza Nobre Lamarão

Introduction

The problem of street children in Belém, a Brazilian city of about 1.5 million people, is by no means as great as in São Paulo, Rio de Janeiro, and Recife. However, there is such a dearth of information about a worldwide and ever-growing phenomenon that, while we make no claim to great expertise in the matter, we believe that our material may be of use to anyone considering this type of work. We were able to become involved only thanks to altruistic friends and understanding relatives in Brazil, through whose help we were able to work within what is termed 'the popular movement'. Our experience owes everything to the energy, ability, and commitment of many different people.

Our involvement was mainly with adolescent girls and young children (about whom even less is known than about boys) through our attachment to the Centro de Defensa do Menor — CDM (Centre for the Defence of the Child). The CDM consists of student and graduate social workers, lawyers and psychologists; it is a branch of the Républica do Pequeno Vendedo (The Young Street Vendors' Association), which in turn is allied to the national movement for street children (Movimento Nacional de Meninas e Meninos da Rua).

Who are the street children?

When we refer to street children, we mean children who spend all day on the street. Some of them remain there at night, some have homes, others drift in and out of the houses of families, relatives, employees, and friends. With the constant movement from country to town, the number of street children is increasing. Today, it includes not only adolescent boys, but adolescent girls, young children and, at times, whole families.

Nobody knows exactly how many there are: estimates vary widely. Some official bodies seek to cover up the extent of the problem. Other groups involved in the provision of care seek to shock by exaggeration, perhaps in the hope of alerting the public and pushing the authorities into more positive action. The situation is already very shocking and needs no exaggeration.

All parties agree that the problem is growing and a solution remains to be found. For many reasons, social care is inadequate in coverage and structure. This, and the more recent appearance of *justiceiros* — vigilantes and extermination squads who, often with the approval of shopkeepers, businessmen, and the police, are attempting to 'solve' the problem by murder, has added to the sense of alienation, fear, and mistrust felt by children who already live on the edge of society.

Working with street children is frustrating; goals are often poorly defined and results nebulous. Even the removal of a child from the streets into a family environment does not constitute complete success. Such are the scars of the past that it is arguable whether many of them can ever adapt and reintegrate themselves into society. Many are rightly ambivalent about whether they wish to return. They mostly left home because of parental violence and rejection, and the precarious camaraderie, excitement, and independence offered by the streets bears no comparison to life as it was at home. They have no role model for stability and affection, and so find it hard to demonstrate these qualities. They are suspicious, inconsistent, and unreliable. One might ask: 'Who can blame them?', but many obviously do.

Most street children have had little or no formal education. In Brazil only 10 per cent of all children currently complete primary school education; and it was rare for us to find any who had studied beyond the most elementary level. After living on the streets, it is very difficult for a child to return to formal school teaching. The strict discipline of many schools contrasts with the volatile, disruptive nature of these children; and habitual glue sniffing does not enhance concentration on a curriculum which is at times wholly inappropriate. If asked, most children will glibly reply that they would love to study. Others might reflect that they would like to learn something relevant to getting a job. Many have already been expelled from school and would face the same fate if they ever got round to going back.

Small children of 4 or 5 usually go on to the streets with older brothers or sisters. Those who begin street life alone are usually between the ages of 7 and 15. The boys do occasional work, like watching and washing parked cars and shoe-shining — although they can find themselves competing with adults trying to do the same job. The girls are more likely to be street vendors, selling sweets and chewing gum. Many of the boys drift into theft and the girls into prostitution. However, they almost always express a desire to work, and do not generally boast about stealing. Many have been in employment on market stalls or as live-in maids, but left due to exploitation.

They tend to hang around in groups of six or so; and a degree of collective loyalty builds up, usually directed against external forces like the police. In Belém, street children are sought out by the fundamentalist evangelical church and occasionally social services — as well as by tourists who want photographs of them.

Virtually all the children have also been picked up by the police and suffered beatings and extortion. Some are released only on condition that they return with more stolen goods. A 1991 statute forbade the police to arrest any minor simply on the suspicion of theft. But the police, who are poorly paid, and even more poorly trained, continue to do so. For example, we arrived once at the children's usual hangout to find that practically all males in the group had been taken into custody. Apparently, since the next day was Mothers' Day, and the streets were crowded with shoppers, these boys would be released only after the shops had closed. Such action is very common and meets with approval from shop owners and shoppers alike. Phrases like 'fine-toothed comb operation' are used when the police remove the 'lice' from the streets before any large festival, holiday, or the arrival of an important politician.

It is not entirely surprising that a study by the Fundacão do Bem Estar do Menor found that 30 per cent of street children had ambitions to be policemen, because they would then be able to rob freely without fear of being caught and beaten up (Dimenstein 1992). The reality is that 60 per cent of Sao Paulo's prison inmates were once street children. Such candid admissions pepper the street children's views on life. Most use glue and cannabis when they can. In a CDM survey,[1] when asked what he thought of drug addiction, one youth replied that he thought it was great when you could finance your addiction, but a bit rough when you couldn't.

Survival strategies on the street

Theft becomes a way of life especially for the boys, just as prostitution does for many of the girls. When they don't make enough money from washing or watching parked cars, shining shoes, or selling chewing gum, they look for alternatives. Yet the suspicion with which adults view them, often a consequence of having been victims of petty and sometimes violent crime, is dwarfed by the fear these children have of adults. We are the ones who abuse them, force them into becoming unwilling sexual partners, deny them access to any rights they may have on paper. We can have them picked up, locked up, beaten up. Some of us can even have them killed. Mutual mistrust precludes any attempt to gain insight and only serves to provide fertile ground for the vigilantes and their radical 'solutions'.

Prostitution

Just as all street boys are presumed to be thieves, all street girls are generally presumed to be prostitutes. Girls of 12 and 13 will often be offered money or gifts in exchange for sexual favours. Customers will harass them, saying: 'I won't buy any of your chewing gum, but I'll buy you.' If the girl reacts with a strongly-worded rejection, this only serves to reinforce the customers' belief that 'She's no virgin'. If they do eventually become prostitutes, albeit initially on an irregular basis, they will discuss it in third-party terms: 'A friend of mine went with such and such ...', or '... she wasn't selling any sweets that day, so you can't blame her, although I wouldn't go with a man for money ...'. Though girls might earn more money, prostitution is not seen as a positive step by them. There is no sense of pride in their independence as prostitutes. These girls are not in control of their destiny. It is an act of desperation, and they are (and see themselves as) victims.

Coupled with the precocious sexual activity which takes place among the children themselves is a high level of ignorance and mis-information about bodily functions, sexually transmitted diseases, conception, contraception, and abortion. Early pregnancy, some-times accompanied by misguided attempts at abortion, becomes inevitable. Perhaps because of this inevitability, or simply as a means of coping, girls rarely display any despair — or for that matter joy — when they realise that they are pregnant. These young girls are not mentally equipped for motherhood. The baby, when it arrives, will be treated like the doll they never had; cuddled and caressed and dressed up prettily (if possible) and then discarded when boredom or irritation sets in.

Street girls often return home or go to a relative's or friend's house at the time of the birth. But they rarely stay off the streets for long. A couple of weeks after the birth, they will be back, leaving the child in the care of a relative or other children. They have no appropriate role model for motherhood, and rarely a good mother substitute. Breast-feeding is a non-starter, vaccination unlikely. The street is a habit very difficult to kick.

The girls' apparent acceptance of the inevitable is reflected in their reaction if the child dies. Few lessons are learned from the past. We met the mother of a street girl who told us how her second grandson had just died from measles. The vaccine is available in Brazil, albeit on an irregular basis. 'That's funny,' she said. 'His big brother died of that too.' Another girl of 8, whose mother came to the streets daily, organising the boys into theft and the girls into selling, told us of the recent death of her stepbrother just days before his first birthday. 'We were going to have a party,' she said, 'but, well, there's no point in having it if the baby's already dead.'

Boys, who have often fathered a couple of children by the age of 16 or so, remain boys. Although proud of this apparent virility, they much prefer kicking a ball, or flying a kite made of old plastic bags, or larking around at the docks with their friends, to active parenthood. They are no more ready for it than the girls are; in many ways, their ignorance makes them more immature than boys of their age in more privileged circumstances.

Street children often express a romantic view of family life as it is for others, with beautiful caring parents, attractive loving children, and no arguments, let alone any violence. This naiveté is also expressed in other things like their views on sexual relations. For example, we were once reading through a picture book on sex, a book written for middle-class adolescents which described a dreamy, romantic, and eventually orgasmic experience between two consenting adults. Knowing that many of these children had suffered rape and sexual abuse, one of us asked somewhat irritatedly, 'But is this what it's really like for you? Is this *your* reality?' 'Of course it is,' they replied. 'How else could it be?' This romanticism may be another defence mechanism; and, if so, very understandable. Such are the harsh realities of life on the street that if they were constantly to confront them, in the knowledge that there is very little they can alter, these children would surely not last very long. It was a mistake for us, with no such dilemma, to try and force them to do so.

Although there are some loners, street children generally take part in many shared activities: glue-sniffing, cannabis smoking, playing, bathing, selling, and stealing. Prostitution is sometimes, especially initially, carried out in pairs. Unless they have a steady partner, girls who remain on the street at night tend to sleep separately from boys, to avoid unwanted sexual contact.

Crime, peddling, and begging

We met some families, like the one mentioned above, living a Dickensian existence — the mother usually in the role of Fagin. Theft is a grab-and-run affair from shops, or from shoppers who are wearing watches and necklaces. Some older girls organise their younger siblings into selling sweets and chewing gum. The younger the child, the more likely she is to meet with public sympathy and, therefore, the more likely the sell to be successful. Girls usually buy a large box of sweets or chewing gum and go around the bars and restaurants selling the contents individually. If they do well, they will make 100 per cent profit, half of which is used to restock. On a good day they earn about £2.00. Since the minimum salary is currently about £30.00 per month, if they manage £2.00, they are pleased. But good days are few and far between. Shoe-

shining can bring in a similar income, but requires a greater initial investment in a box, polish, and brushes (plus or minus a chair), which puts it beyond the reach of many boys. Begging is another means of earning money or, more usually, food. Tourists and lunchtime diners in cafés and restaurants are frequently accosted with pleas of 'Buy me a sandwich?' or 'Are you going to finish that?'

Subject to abuse, threats, and insults as they are, street children have very low self-esteem and a low opinion of their peers or anyone else who differs from society's perceived norm. Thus they can themselves be very racist, reactionary, and bigoted. Once, to assist with a discussion on contraception we used a flannelgraph which, being originally designed for use in Africa, had African figures. The street girls reacted with laughter and abuse at 'those weird, unfashionably dressed blacks'. Perhaps one of the reasons why we ourselves managed to get on well was that our fair-skinned, fair-haired, middle-class, educated *gringo* image was one to which, sadly, they aspired.

We made many friends among the street children and grew to trust several. However, we never wore watches when we went to meet them and carried very little money. The 'live for today' urge in these children, built up over many years, is so strong that it would be foolish to expect them not to capitalise on a golden opportunity. And anyway, why should they trust us to be around for ever? We learned these lessons from the best helpers in our group, who had learnt that the best results were based not just on friendship, but on understanding.

Although these children share the same aspirations as other children, they say they enjoy life on the streets. They like to be able to do what they want, to play football, to fish, fly a kite, hang around, laugh and joke. But they also say that they want to leave it for a proper family life, for support and help, for love and affection.

The results of the first survey by CDM make disturbing reading.[2] No doubt the results of the second survey, when completed, will be similar. We have quoted freely from these surveys in the course of writing this article.

Our aims and methods

The CDM was founded in the early 1980s by members of its parent organisation, The Young Street Vendors' Association. It functions in two ways: it deals with individual cases referred for help; and it acts as an information centre on street children, street vendors, and the 'popular movement'. This is done through regular literature searches, with updates of the CDM library and self-initiated surveys, sometimes in conjunction with other groups.

Individual cases are referred by teachers and educators, parents, the children themselves, the courts and, sometimes, the police. Until this project began, most of the casework resulted from these referrals. Each case is discussed at a case conference by a team of students and practising sociologists, psychologists, and lawyers, who decide what each division should do and the practical steps required: home visits, meetings with the police, etc.

The staff realised that by dealing only with referrals, CDM was attending to only a small part of the overall need. This was confirmed by interviews with street children, many of whom did not know of the existence of CDM. Part of the problem was the location of the Centre itself which (because the building had been a donation) was situated a few miles from the city centre, in a middle-class neighbourhood.

Then a large interview-based study by CDM identified a new, escalating problem of street girls who had little support and were often suffering the effects of prostitution, sexually transmitted diseases, and early pregnancy. This study made a number of recommendations which involved commencing outreach work. The particular project on which we worked was started with the intention of completing some of the recommendations. These were:

1 To make ourselves available on the streets and meet the street girls in an attempt to interest them in a programme of activities and discussions related to and chosen by them.

2 To make ourselves available to attend to the tangible needs of the street girls such as first aid, legal problems, social and psychological problems, inter-group conflicts and, if possible, ante-natal care.

3 To begin an intensive programme of self-esteem building to counteract the downward spiral of these children.

First contacts

After extensive planning and meetings, we began the process of getting to know the street children. This involved regular visits to the areas where these children hang out (mainly the docks and markets), making ourselves known to them, buying them the occasional meal, and trying to gain their trust. In this we relied on Maria Luiza Nobre Lamarão (Lu), who was the driving force behind the project and already knew many of the girls; and Denise, an ex-street girl who was, amazingly, just about to enter university.

The first time we (Scanlon and Scanlon) stood around at the docks, after dark, trying to talk with glue-sniffing children, our mistrust (we too had been victims of petty crime) turned into the considerable fear that we were being very foolish and were just about to find out why. We felt particularly marked by being *gringos*. Many of the children eyed us up suspiciously. Fortunately, we were spared any humiliation. 'You can take your hands out of your pockets, uncle,' one of them said. 'If we'd wanted to rob you, we'd have done it long ago.' There were times when we moved away, or doubled back because an area became unsafe, or there were some unknown children behaving threateningly. However, on the whole we had few problems.

Our aim was to provide a setting where we could meet with the street children, initially on a minimum weekly basis for discussion and to attend to their practical problems, most of which had already been clearly defined by the girls themselves at a meeting held in the CDM office the previous year. Our initial base was small, cramped and hot, with too few chairs under a tin roof. This soon sapped any desire to stay awake and talk. It was also too far away from where the children hung out. The enterprising coordinator managed to obtain the use of a large room and garden in a conference centre owned by the archdiocese, right on the dockfront. This proved ideal, since we soon discovered that we needed considerable space: the children were noisy, boisterous, and liked to move around.

We initially targeted the adolescent girls, and set about designing a programme of discussions on street life, contraception, pregnancy, sexually transmitted diseases, etc. However, with food and first aid freely available, it soon wasn't just the teenage girls who came along, but their male friends and young children under their care. Adults sometimes came too. At first, we were unable to see the value of having young children, and merely tried to keep them entertained with crayons and paper while we dealt with the adolescents. However, it became clear that they were among the most regular attenders, and eventually we woke up to the opportunity we had.

Building self-esteem

Having already worked in schools with child-to-child material, where older children explore through activities how to look after their younger siblings better, we had translated a good range of material on health topics like water, diarrhoea, personal hygiene, and so on. However, this material was aimed at children who had some semblance of ordinary family life. The young street children were not in that position and we realised that to address health topics straightaway was premature.

Since these children were victims of daily physical and verbal abuse, they had come to the conclusion that they did indeed make a negative contribution to society. They viewed their plight as entirely the fault of themselves and their parents. They had come to believe what people said about them. How could we conceivably hope to help them to help themselves, if they perceived themselves as worthless? The starting point had to be a specific project to develop the children's self-esteem, asking questions such as:

- Who am I?
- What are my talents, my problems?
- What makes me an individual, different from everyone else, and a valuable part of society?

With adolescents we would often address the question 'Why is it so?', but with the younger ones we stuck to *who* and *what*. We started this with child-to-child tactics using games, activities, drawings, discussions, and stories.

For example, to answer the question *Who am I?*, we made a large poster with a section for each young child. They each completed this section with their name and nickname (we wrote it for them), their hand print and footprint, family details, likes and dislikes, where they lived, and their job/what they did. When a new child came along, s/he completed her details.

Another method was to make a large collage with photographs of all sorts of people in it — beautiful, ugly, rich, poor, old, young, people behaving with violence, people behaving with compassion — and to encourage the children to pick out their favourites and least favourites, and say why. In other words, trying to establish an identity through positive and negative identification with others.

For continued use throughout the programme, we devised games like 'Pass the ball', with first of all each child shouting the name of someone, then passing the ball to her. Then the same game would be played using nicknames, then descriptions. Another game was a sort of 'What's my line?' where the children had to pretend to be one of their friends, while the others tried to guess their identity through a series of questions. Before we left, we were working on 'The Rights of the Child and Adolescent', the recently-enacted statute, and how to introduce this to the children through stories and booklets.

Talking about health

Having sown these ideas of self-esteem, it was not then so inappropriate to move on to other topics such as the body and the changes that occur at adolescence, personal hygiene (skin, teeth, eyes), food and drink, common illnesses, and habits (smoking, drugs and alcohol). Each session followed the basic child-to-child structure, starting with an objective/idea, followed by some information, and ending with activities. For example:

Teeth

Objective: To understand how to care for our teeth and why it is important.

Information: The uses of teeth; eating, speaking, attractiveness. Milk teeth versus permanent teeth. (We did not discuss molars versus incisors, etc., viewing that as too complicated). What dental caries is, what causes it, and how to prevent it.

Activities: Looking at each other's teeth; the children who sold and chewed gum invariably had the most caries. How to make a home-made toothbrush and toothpaste. Defacing pictures of smiling soap-stars and discussing their appearance before and after. (This proved very popular.) Rewarding them with a free toothpaste and toothbrush. (Not in contradiction to teaching them to make their own, since most were in fact nowhere near being so well motivated.)

Each session was based on a common set of principles: they were informal, two-way, and designed to be delivered in 30-45 minutes, since the children's attention span was short and they were easily distracted. Each session was complete with a beginning, middle, and end: regular attendance was not guaranteed, and so we couldn't rely on information retained from the previous week's session.

We made maximum use of activities and teaching materials, and often intervened to help the children to achieve a good result, for example in drawing. Due to lack of practice, the motor skills of many of them were below average, and it was important that each child achieved and didn't lose face. If this involved a bit of cheating, so what? Each session was designed to cater for the lowest level of skill. Competition was not encouraged, so as to avoid arguments, and once again to encourage a sense of achievement. We were quite happy to take small steps.

The children's response

The adolescent boys, like the young children, had not been specifically targeted, and therefore also took us by surprise. They were the most irregular attenders. Our most frequent personal contact with them was on the street itself, or whenever we patched them up after a beating, fight or stabbing. When they did come, they usually chatted with the male law students of CDM, since their problems were often with the police. We did undertake a programme to make them more aware of their rights in the light of the new statute, and how best they might achieve them in practice. Due to the legal complexities and the practical difficulties involved, this was a longer-term initiative, which was still underway when we left.

The adolescent girls came regularly, although we always went to remind them before each meeting. When the República do Pequeno Vendedor carried out a survey of street children in the mid-1970s, there were virtually no girls. Now they are almost as numerous as the boys, although fewer of them actually live on the streets. Many of them have worked as live-in maids for middle-class families, but left due to ill-treatment. They share many of the same problems: drug abuse, physical and verbal abuse, victimisation, and marginalisation. They have, in addition, their own particular problems: sexual abuse, precocious pregnancy, childbirth and motherhood, a higher risk of sexually transmitted disease, and prostitution. Among the street children of Belem, female prostitution is much more common than male prostitution.

The adolescent girls showed the same feelings of worthlessness and poor self-esteem as the younger children. Although we did not address this in the same direct form, it was the underlying theme of all the meetings. In addition to the food and first aid generally available, we offered these girls a basic ante-natal service. It consisted mainly of the diagnosis of pregnancy, regular physical examination, and a post-natal 'home' visit. We did on occasions arrange urine and blood tests, but our resources were limited. However, we did have contact with a state-funded group helping young prostitutes. This group had access to micro-biological laboratory analyses, which were useful to us, since many of the girls suffered from sexually transmitted diseases. As an incentive, the group offered a free ante-natal service with a built-in reward system of nappies, baby clothes, dummies, and feeding bottles for regular attendance.

Although providing good physical care, the clinic did not provide much in the way of support or education. Strongly-worded directives to 'Breast-feed!' would be accompanied by a free feeding bottle. In fairness, breast-feeding was not favoured by the street girls — although it merited more consideration than a sternly-delivered instruction. We did discuss breast-feeding with the street girls, and came to the conclusion that if the mother was determined to be back on the streets two weeks *post-partum*, then the best solution was to encourage partial breast-feeding and show them, preferably in their own homes, how to make up bottle feeds correctly.

The girls would not breast-feed because, they said, it was not practical: it wasn't compatible with being on the streets all day, and how else were they going to earn any money? And they believed that breast-feeding would result in flat, droopy breasts. Not surprisingly, given the circumstances of the conception, pregnancy, and birth, there appeared to us to be a lack of bonding between mother and infant — and no doubt that was a factor too.

Many of our discussions with these girls centred around sexual matters such as puberty, menstruation, contraception, vaginal discharge, and sexually transmitted diseases. We would also talk about general topics like drugs, personal hygiene, street life, basic rights and how to deal with the police, or about the work of the National Movement of Street Children.

We used videos, slides, flannelgraphs, booklets and stories. The adolescent boys and girls enjoyed drawing as much as the younger children did, so we employed this method too. There was no set format to the discussions, but the same fundamental principles used with the younger children were also applied here. Underlying each session was the theme of 'I am an individual and a valuable asset to society', and the question 'Why is the situation we live in like it is?' The videos from the National Movement of Street Children made by children themselves, with a specific focus on these matters, made a particularly strong impression on the girls, as well as on us.

Street girls: two cases

'Success' in this work has to be measured in very modest terms. A typical case is that of a 15-year-old girl who, with her brothers and sisters, had been working on the streets for several years. She was encouraged to do so by her mother, who had several children by two different fathers in two different houses, and was consequently glad to see the back of some of them. This girl would more often go home in the evening than remain on the streets.

She became pregnant, stating that the father was a street boy, and was encouraged to attend the group for young prostitutes referred to above. The baby's father actually attended with her on some visits. She received at the same time advice and basic ante-natal care from CDM, and regularly attended our meetings. She gave birth successfully, and we visited her at home to congratulate her and to offer advice on child care. About ten days after the baby was born, she returned to the streets to resume selling chewing gum, leaving the baby at home in the care of siblings and a grandmother who was intermittently available.

When we left, she said that she was still breast-feeding morning and night (three months *post-partum*), and we knew that she was going home in the evenings. The father continued to show an interest in his child, and often stayed with the girl at night. We met them both regularly on the streets. She continued to attend our meetings, had learned something about contraception, and was just about to start taking the pill.

At the other end of the spectrum we had frequent contact with a pregnant 14-year-old, but only once persuaded her to come along to our meeting place, where she had an ante-natal examination. She had left home because of parental violence, and remained for most of the day with the baby's father. He was 16, and every time we met him he was confused and sniffing glue. She slept on the streets. We arranged to take her to an appointment at the centre for young prostitutes, but before this we visited her on the streets to confirm the date, time, and meeting place with her.

On that occasion she was very tearful and reluctant to speak. Tears are not a common occurrence among street children. Her boyfriend was sniffing glue and unable to enlighten us. While we were talking to her, she excused herself, saying she wanted to use the public toilets. She went there crying, and never came back. We never saw her again, and although we heard that she had successfully given birth, we were unable to trace her or to find out with certainty what had happened to her.

On leaving

Working with street children can be very depressing. The situation is not getting any better, and it's easy to feel helpless and hopeless. The real answer, of course, lies not in programmes like the one we were involved with, but in large-scale social changes resulting in greater equity worldwide. To achieve this, we need first to develop a global vision. Perhaps that is beginning to emerge.

We felt a mixture of guilt and sadness on leaving Brazil. The work with CDM and the street children was immensely rewarding, although it probably brought the fewest concrete results of all the work we did. Our confused feelings were compounded by the gratitude expressed by the children to their Uncle and Aunty Gringo; such is the economic reality of life in Brazil that we did after all leave them in a worse state than they were when we first arrived.

We were once asked if we thought we had achieved anything of value in Brazil that is continuing in our absence. The short answer is, probably no. Our role was to give impetus and momentum to the many Brazilians already working in these areas and committed to years of active participation. They are the ones who will find their own solutions. We believe that is how it should be.

Notes

1 'Diagnostico sobre a Situacao dos Meninos(as) que moram nas Ruas de Belém.' An analysis of the current state of the street children of Belém. Centro de Defesa do Menor (Coordinator, Katia Macedo).

2 'Cotidiano de Miseria e Formas de Exploracao Sexual de Meninas em Belém' ('The Daily Catalogue of Misery and Sexual Exploitation of Young Girls in Belém'). Movimento Républica do Pequeno Vendedor and Centro de Defesa do Menor. By Maria Luiza Nobre Lamarão, Maria Bernadete Santos Oliveira, and Rosa Elizabeth Acevedo Marin. Available from the Institute of Child Health, University of London, 30 Guildford Street, London.

References

Dimenstein, Gilberto, 1992, *Brazil: War on Children*, London: Latin America Bureau.

The authors

Maria Luiza Nobre Lamarão is a sociologist who works with a research and information department of the University of Para in Belém. One of the founder members of CDM, she is coordinating a paper-recycling programme with street children.

Tom Scanlon is a medical doctor with a background in general practice, currently working as a senior registrar in South West Thames Public Health Medicine Department, based at St George's Hospital in London.

Francesca Scanlon is a medical doctor training in psychiatry and currently on the St George's Psychiatric Registrar Rotation. Together with her husband Tom, she spent two years working in Brazil in 'popular health', mainly through the Young Street Vendors' Association. Specific projects involved child to child work with schoolchildren, women's health with women's groups, ante-natal care with the state service, and latterly street children with the CDM.

This article first appeared in *Development in Practice*, Volume 3, Number 1, in 1993.

Older people and development: the last minority?

Mark Gorman

Introduction

It is now well recognised that the populations of the industrialised countries of Europe and North America inhabit an ageing society, as the numbers and proportions of older people grow rapidly. Major advances in medicine and health care have improved nutrition and reduced the incidence of infectious disease.

Rising living standards, together with better education, health care, and social services, have contributed to dramatic increases in longevity over the past century. Because these changes occurred first in the North, there is a tendency to associate 'population ageing'[1] only with these countries. However, countries of the South already account for more than half the world's population aged 60 or over. By the year 2025, this proportion will have risen to about 70 per cent.[2] The steady and sustained growth of older populations, which already poses a considerable challenge to policy-makers in the North, also needs to be recognised as an important issue in the South, one which will profoundly affect economies and societies.

The demographic transition

A global demographic transition is thus clearly under way, though it has reached a more advanced stage in the North than the South. Non-industrialised countries of the South continue to have a high proportion of children and a relatively low proportion of older people in their populations. In developing countries as a whole, approximately 35 per cent of populations are under 15 years and about 10 per cent are over 55, while in the North the proportions are approximately equal, at about 22 per cent (Kinsella and Taeuber, 1993). It is, therefore, not surprising that attention continues to concentrate on the growth in numbers of young people, rather than on growth among the older populations.

However, evidence of the demographic transition is increasingly visible in the developing world. Many countries in Asia and Latin America experienced substantial declines in fertility during the 1970s, and the trends are projected to become stronger. Asia, for example, had 48 per cent of the global total of older people in 1985, and will have 58 per cent by 2025. By contrast, the corresponding figures for Europe are 20 per cent and 12 per cent. In sub-Saharan Africa, the phenomenon of ageing populations is still in its early stages; here too the pattern could be replicated (Schulz, 1991), though the impact of the AIDS pandemic will clearly affect this process. Even in countries where life-expectancy at birth remains relatively low, life-expectancy at the age of 65 can be surprisingly high. In Bangladesh, for example, where life-expectancy at birth for women was recorded as 54.7 years in 1984, at the age of 65 the average woman's life-expectancy was a further 12.8 years. In Sri

Lanka in 1981, the comparable figures for women were 71.6 years at birth and a further 15.6 years at the age of 65. This compares with the 1985 figure of life-expectancy for Japanese women aged 65 of 18.9 more years. The common expectation for people in south Asia is another 10 to 15 years of life from the age of 65 (Martin, 1990).

The demographic transition now being experienced in the South differs in important respects from the pattern of industrialised countries. In developing countries, reductions in birth and death rates have been achieved less by the socio-economic improvements which were a feature of Europe and North America over the past century and more by technological innovations (such as mass vaccination campaigns) amid continuing poverty. The prospect therefore is one of rapidly increasing numbers of older people who will live out their last years with few of the social, economic, and health-care support systems available in the North.

Not only will the older populations of all countries rise dramatically, but they will become increasingly heterogeneous, in common with the experience of the rest of the population. The oldest old (those over 80) are the fastest-growing component of older populations all over the world, and the numbers of older people with a disability are likewise growing rapidly. A recent projection for Indonesia shows a rapid increase in the numbers of people over the age of 45 with a physical handicap,[3] as higher rates of prevalence over that age combine with population growth. Thus the number of women over 45 with a handicap is projected to rise nearly fourfold, to 7.1 million by 2025 (Dowd and Manton, 1992). The increasing dependence of these groups will have a significant impact on family care-giving, particularly with the global decline in public-service provision. Given the propensity of women to marry younger and to outlive men in nearly all societies, they are much more likely to be living alone in old age, with greatly reduced socio-economic support. Migration, both internal and international, is now a global phenomenon, and is creating large pockets of older people, either left behind in rural areas, or concentrated in urban slums. Life for older people in both cases is often characterised by low incomes, substandard housing, and inadequate services (Sen, 1993).

Theories of ageing and development

Much of the debate in the small but growing literature on ageing and development has focused on the status of older people, and hence the roles which they are perceived to be assigned or denied in societies undergoing change. In general terms, two broad theoretical frameworks have been established.

Modernisation theory

Modernisation theory, so influential in other areas of development thinking, has had a pervasive effect on comparative gerontology also. In summary, it propounds the view that 'modernisation often sets in motion a chain reaction which tends to undermine the status of the aged'. Features of this process are said to be the decline in importance of the extended family and the decline in land ownership as a resource of high status; increasing social and geographical mobility; and rapid changes in social and cultural structures and values. The family values and respect for old people found in traditional societies are set against the 'modernising' values of individualism, the work ethic, and 'a cosmopolitan outlook which emphasises efficiency and progress' (Cowgill, 1986).

Whether modernisation is viewed positively or negatively, this positing of opposing poles characterising 'traditional' and 'modern' societies attracts much support among writers on ageing and development. On the one hand a nostalgic view of traditional societies is drawn: 'In our traditional social system, old age was considered wisdom personified, the fruit of a well-spent life, and commanded unquestionable power, authority and respect. The security of the joint family was a reassurance for the elderly' (Kaur *et al*, 1987).

In contrast, modernisation is seen as undermining this golden age. Two comments on migration and urbanisation illustrate a recurrent theme. Migration, for example, 'has helped to turn the economic modernisation of developing countries into a social nightmare for older people' (Tout, 1989). Again, 'It seems as though no tradition is able to resist one generation of urban life. The disintegration of the family along with urbanisation — especially when it is unmanaged — weakens religious sentiment and brings about the disappearance of respect for elderly people' (Jacquemin, 1993).

Dependency theory

Modernisation theory has not, however, gone unchallenged. A number of critiques have been made, notably that by Neysmith and Edwardh. They argue from the perspective of dependency theory, and say 'economic dependency spawns an ideology which blames underdevelopment on the characteristics of people, rather than on the economic relations which bind the third world to the industrial world' (Neysmith and Edwardh, 1984). They, and others, have argued that demographic factors such as the number of surviving children, and economic factors such as class, occupation, and ownership of assets play a far more significant role than is assigned to them by a concentration on universal status or value systems. Any loss of status on the part of older people is more likely to have been 'linked to ingrained structural inequalities experienced by most people in most developing countries in earlier life. Impoverishment in old age may be a common cross-cultural experience of the ageing process, rather than simply resulting from "modernisation"' (Sen, 1993).

This debate clearly has important practical implications for development activity with

older people. If, as modernisation theory implies, older people in the South lead secure and fulfilled lives because they still live in extended family settings, there is arguably little need for intervention by governments or NGOs. However, if the forces of modernisation are undermining traditional cultural values and thus eroding family care, support for older people may be needed, but could concentrate on a 'welfarist' approach, particularly on the institutionalisation of those outside family care systems.

If, on the other hand, the problems faced by older people are seen in the context of structural inequalities both between societies and within them, the concentration should be on care and support models focused at community level, while developing a critique of the unequal relationships which affect older people in common with other vulnerable social groups. It is, therefore, important to examine the evidence for the validity of these competing theories. Much debate has centred on older people and the changing role of the family in the South, and this is where we start.

Older people and the family

In most countries of the South (and indeed the North), the key socio-economic relationship for the great majority of older people is the family. Within the family, the mutuality of obligations between the generations facilitates an exchange of support and care. Thus child-minding by grandparents for their working children is exchanged for care and protection of the older family members. The idea of the family has a powerful, even emotive influence on many. It is often asserted that the traditional extended family structure provides adequate care and support for the great majority of older people. However, another commonly held view is that the extended family support mechanism is increasingly threatened by the transition from a traditional to a modern society.

The evidence, though so far partial, points to a more complex reality. It is certainly the case that the extended family still plays a major part in supporting older family members, even where rapid socio-economic change is taking place. However, extended family support is often insufficient to guarantee a reasonable quality of life in old age. In sub-Saharan Africa, for instance, the majority of older people still receive primary support from their families, both in rural and urban areas. For example, surveys of four West African nations conducted between 1985 and 1988 found that about 80 per cent of respondents over the age of 60 were receiving help from children or grandchildren (Peil quoted in Cattell, 1990).

In south Asia too, most older people still live within extended family settings, and again this is true in both urban and rural situations. Evidence from Bangladesh, India, and Nepal indicates that most older South Asians live with their (usually male) children, and the same study provides clear evidence of continued feelings of affection and duty which seem to contradict the idea that family structures are necessarily undermined by rapid social change (Martin, 1990).

However, it is equally clear that family relations are affected by a wide range of socio-economic factors, and that these factors, though they may be exacerbated by social change, have not been caused by them. There is, for example, evidence to indicate that the social status of older people has always been linked to their economic power, whether in 'traditional' or 'modern' settings. A study of older people within their family settings in Nepal concluded that social and economic changes have not caused a decline in the status of older people, but simply brought to the surface underlying inter-generational conflict, by altering the balance of the powerful socio-economic forces which traditionally acted as a restraint (Goldstein, Schuler and Ross, 1983).

Conflict between generations

This situation is significantly worsened by the increasing poverty of many families in the South. The inter-generational tension which is frequently noted in multi-generational families in the developing world is often ascribed to changing cultural values arising from the transition from traditional to modern societies. However, it seems much more likely that it is poverty, not modernising forces, which is the prime cause of this family tension. Commenting on the family situation of migrant workers in one of the *pueblos jóvenes* (new towns) surrounding Lima, a report notes that 'where elderly people live with their adult children, the presence of an extra person strains the limited resources of the family, reinforcing the elderly people's view of themselves as a burden' (HelpAge International, 1993a).

It is also important to recognise that care for older people in the extended family is not a responsibility that is equally shared. Discussion of the enduring quality of family care often ignores the fact that this duty falls disproportionately on younger female household members. Throughout the world, the bulk of informal care of older people is undertaken by women, in addition to the responsibilities they undertake for their husbands and children. This situation is worsened in the South (and increasingly in the North too) by the lack of external support through social and health services, and by poverty, so that, even within families willing to care for older people, there is a hidden crisis of care-giving.

Older people and their communities

What is true of the experience of older people in the family is also true of their relationship with the community. Again the belief that chronological age traditionally confers an automatic status on older people is not borne out by the evidence. A study of older people in a Punjabi village found that fewer than one-third of men aged 60 or more were members of the village organisations, and of these the overwhelming majority were under the age of

70. The conclusion that 'participation in village organisation was influenced directly by economic factors and education', and not by chronological age or wisdom, is echoed in other studies (Sharma and Dak, 1987).

The marginalisation experienced by older people is even greater for those who lack substantial property, and therefore have no resources to deploy to ensure care and security from family or community in old age. This is especially true for older women, often widows whose property has been distributed to their sons when their husbands die. For many women in developing countries, the descent into total dependency begins with the death of the husband. This special vulnerability of older women is of particular concern, not least because of their rapidly growing numbers, since women are likely to form an increasing proportion of the older population, as life-expectancy increases at a faster rate among women than men. Again, a high proportion of older women are widows, and this proportion increases with age. It has been said that widowhood is a fact of life for women over 75 in the South. There were 21.5 million older widows in China in 1990, far more than the combined total for the countries of the European Union (Kinsella, 1993). For women who have never married, or who are childless, the situation is even more desperate, and in many societies an old age lived out in destitution is assured.

Older people's health

A crucial measure of well-being for older people is that of their health status. It has long been recognised that, given the profound mutual effects of poverty and health status, efforts to improve people's health play a central role in the development process. This is again even more the case for the health of older people. We have seen that the developing world is in effect experiencing a process of ageing because of the prevention of premature death from infectious disease, not because of factors such as rising affluence,

better housing, or improved nutrition. Some infectious diseases such as TB or dysentery remain widespread, and intestinal and respiratory infections experienced in earlier years are significant causes of morbidity and loss of active life in later years. The arduous lifestyles of the great majority of people in the South significantly worsen this situation. A review of older people's health in the developing world at the beginning of the 1990s concluded:

The broad international evidence seems clear that, from a health perspective, those over 60 in Third and Fourth World nations are unlikely to be living in geriatric utopias. Rather, they are more likely living in endemic areas of debilitating diseases, where inadequate housing and water supplies increase the likelihood of frequent reinfection, and inadequate diets lower resistance to illness-causing microbes. (Sokolovsky, 1991)

Again the effects on older women are particularly severe. The increasing debate over the role of older women in the development process has focused predominantly on the structural inequalities affecting women earlier in life, and ignored the increasing relative disadvantage which they experience as they grow older. Yet it is precisely the accumulating disadvantage of earlier years which makes older women in poverty particularly vulnerable. A woman of 50 in a developing country who has experienced a lifetime of hard physical labour and multiple pregnancies is already at the threshold of old age, and her later life, which may well extend for another 20–30 years, will be profoundly affected by her greatly impaired functional capacity (Kalache, 1991, Rosenmayr, 1991).

The dependence of women in many households (in matters of food allocation, for instance) is a characteristic example of this. Much evidence bears out the findings of a recent study of mid-life and older women in Latin America and the Caribbean. In Guyana a study by the Pan American Health

Organisation (PAHO) of East Indian families found that nutritional status was closely associated with the sex of the child, with boys being healthier. This establishes a lifetime pattern, in which chronic malnutrition and anaemia combine to produce an old age of extreme debility (Sennott-Miller 1989).

Much of the developing world is still characterised by high levels of fertility, but also by significantly declining levels of mortality, and increasing life-expectancy. There is also evidence that health trends in the developing countries are emulating those of the developed world. For example, cardiovascular and cerebral diseases have markedly increased in the industrialising countries of Latin America and South-East Asia (Tout, 1989).

The implications for health-service provision in the South are profound, as the health-care needs increasingly diverge from the services provided. For example, while most older people live in rural areas, much health-service provision is located in the cities. The relative lack of mobility and the poverty of many older rural dwellers effectively deny them access to these services. In the cities, where hospital-based facilities are concentrated, older people do indeed form a large proportion of users. However, to some extent this simply reflects the imbalance in provision between hospital-based and community-based services, and it is the latter which should provide the bulk of health-care to older people. But even where community-based services exist, their priorities rarely include older people. There is an enormous dearth of knowledge of the special health needs of older people in the developing world, and, despite the introduction in recent years of a number of courses, mainly offered by the NGO sector, a profound lack of trained health personnel to work with them.

Income security

The critical variable in the well-being or otherwise of older people is their economic status and their ability to control resources. Today, as in the past, income for consumption needs has come predominantly from work activities, and this remains true for most people, often into very old age, in many countries of the South. However, illness, injury, and unemployment reduce older people's ability to rely on work as a prime source of income. Nevertheless, in the absence of comprehensive social-security systems in developing countries, it is not surprising to observe relatively high rates of labour-force participation at older ages. Well over half of men aged 65 or more were still working in countries as widely dispersed as Jamaica, Mexico, Liberia, Pakistan, and Malaysia during the 1980s (Kinsella 1993). Because most older workers are employed in agriculture or other unregulated activity, 'retirement', in so far as it exists, is characterised by a gradual withdrawal from the work force, and increased reliance on other resources. These are, as we have seen, predominantly derived from family support. A study of Fiji, Malaysia, the Philippines, and the Republic of Korea found that typically 40 per cent or more of older people's income came from the family (Andrews *et al.* 1985).

With the growth in underemployment and unemployment among younger people in many countries in the South, older workers' prospects of continued substantial participation in the non-agricultural labour force do not seem good. At the same time, lack of employment prospects will continue to reduce the capacity of younger family members to support their ageing relatives, especially when difficult choices need to be made between providing for their parents or for their own children. 'Given the already difficult choice facing sons regarding the allocation of their meagre income ... and given the inability of poor third world governments ... to mount substantial social service programs, it is likely that more and more elderly people will be unable to live their latter years in a secure and dignified setting' (Goldstein, Schuler and Ross, 1983).

'Hidden' economic and social activities

Again, for older women the problems are compounded. Even the scale of older women's work is unknown. The concentration of older workers (women and men) in agriculture and related sectors, and narrow definitions of what constitutes productive activity, obscure the true picture. Thus the enormous contribution of older women in support of younger relatives through, for example, child-minding and house-keeping is not recorded in analyses of older people's economic activities. Yet these family-support roles often play an important part in household economies. In many rural communities in various parts of the world, increasing numbers of older people take care of the children of a middle generation who have gone to urban centres (or in some cases emigrated) to seek work. A typical case is that of a 73-year old woman in rural Botswana, caring for four grandchildren on behalf of sons and daughters working in South Africa. They seldom come home, and the woman complains that 'There are no good sons nowadays' (Ingstad *et al.*, 1992).

In times of crisis, this role can become crucial. A common, but again little-reported, phenomenon has been the care given by the grandparent generation to children orphaned by the AIDS pandemic in Africa. In some rural communities in Uganda and Zimbabwe, for example, anecdotal evidence provides a picture of almost literal decimation of the middle generation in some communities, leaving orphaned children totally dependent on the grandparent generation. Older parents also play a predominant role in care for people with AIDS. In one district of Mashonaland in Zimbabwe, a study found that the carers 'were all, without exception, elderly women who were sometimes assisted by their younger female relatives' (Jazdowska, 1992).

The participation of older people in the economic life of developing countries is surprisingly pervasive. A significant proportion of city street traders in the developing world are older people. A study of women's work in a Muslim community of northern Nigeria describes a broad range of trading activities undertaken by older women. These include small-scale trade, pawnbroking, and preparation of food for sale. In addition, 'to older women is reserved the practice of particular occupations involving the exercise of ritual power and authority, such as midwifery, the preparation of girls for marriage and of the bodies of women for burial, and the making of herbal medicines' (Coles, 1991). Traditional birth attendants throughout Africa and Asia, particularly in communities where the mobility of women is restricted by cultural norms, are overwhelmingly older women.

Social insurance provision

Pension or income-support schemes which cover any more than a small minority of workforces in most developing countries seem unlikely to be feasible, given their very low levels of economic development. Even in countries where social insurance systems have evolved, such as the People's Republic of China, the coverage remains modest in scale. Programmes cover State-sector workers, but not the nearly three-quarters of the labour force who are rural workers. To compensate for this limited coverage, family support of older relatives has been made a legal requirement. Reforms such as a broadening of the retirement policy and an increasing emphasis on population planning have the potential to exert increasing economic pressures, as the number of retired older people grows (Liu, 1982). This is also true of other developing countries, and the combination of family and community support with self-help remains the most feasible option for the great majority of older people.

Emergency relief services for older people

The way in which economic and social circumstances affect the status of older people is nowhere more starkly illustrated than in situations of disaster or conflict. It has become a media cliché that the worst-affected victims of disasters are the young and the old. However, in contrast to the strong focus on assistance to children from both within and outside disaster-affected communities, older people receive little attention. In part this is certainly because they tend to be extremely self-effacing. It is, for example, characteristic of older refugee-camp inhabitants that they will give their food ration to the whole family — partly at least as a means of demonstrating their continued role as providers — and go without food themselves. The author has witnessed a distribution of clothing to displaced older people in Mozambique at which the queue which formed was entirely made up of children and young adults, while the older people sat together under a tree, literally at the back of the queue. A recent report on the situation of older refugees in Tanzania echoes this situation, noting that older people were finding it difficult to walk to food-distribution points, or to stand for the required two or three hours awaiting food distributions (HelpAge International, 1993b).

The NGO response

NGO projects and programmes focused primarily or exclusively on older people have been few and far between. The relatively small numbers of older people, compared with overall populations, the existence of extended family support systems, or the supposed coverage of older people in programmes serving whole communities are given as rationalisations for this lack of activity. There may also be a feeling that older people are a lower priority than other groups, such as children and those younger adults who are seen as 'economically active', and thus making a contribution to the development process.

Within the community of organisations which are working with older people, activity has in the past concentrated on welfare work with the most frail: an approach derived from

the religious organisations whose objectives are to succour the most needy, notably Catholic orders such as the Little Sisters of the Poor. In more recent years, there has also been a growing focus on the involvement of older people as active participants in a development process. A wide variety of work, from income generation to reminiscence projects, has shown older people's potential for active participation in development. However, there is still much to be done in terms of developing an understanding of the special requirements of project work with older people. It is important, for example, at the beginning of the project cycle, to devise approaches to analysing need which take into account the fact that older people often have a more discursive approach to sharing information. Again, development workers should not underestimate the challenge of finding ways of including older women, who have, as we have seen, often suffered a lifetime's marginalisation. However, the rewards of effective development work with older people can be unexpectedly great. John Mbiizini, a development worker who took part in a workshop on participatory rapid assessment techniques with a group of older farmers in Kenya, described how the use of a seasonality calendar with the group enabled them to plan food production for a year ahead. In describing his work with the group, he said:

... the elderly: one thing, it is very interesting. I found I had company and it was less hectic, it was not tiring, because the elderly really helped. I also found that they really appreciated my being with them to help them. It also helped them to feel that they are part of the solution that we are seeking for the project. (HelpAge International, 1993c)

Conclusion

The development process has been defined as enabling the poorest 'to *have* more (particularly in terms of food and health care) and ... to *be* more, in terms of self-confidence, ability to manage their own future, and improving their status in society at large' (Pratt and Boyden 1985). The central features of this conception of development are not only material improvement but also the participation of all sectors of the population in the development process, as an act of empowerment in itself. What is true of populations as a whole is yet more so for those who are most marginalised among them.

However, powerful factors militate against such involvement. One aspect of the marginalisation of older people in all societies is the negative imagery that is associated with old age. Passivity, inflexibility, and hostility to change are characteristics typically attributed to older people. The contributions made by older people in a wide variety of situations are either ignored or patronisingly sentimentalised. This is also true of the development context. Older people are not usually considered to be part of the development process, since the charac-teristics which they are considered to embody are seen as the antithesis of the development dynamic. They tend to be seen as passive recipients of welfare, with only a short life-expectancy. Hence the almost complete absence of references to the role of older people in the development literature.

We have seen that older people are particularly vulnerable to marginalisation and social isolation, not simply because of features inherent in processes of change, but primarily because of structural inequalities which development aims to transform. It is therefore arguably a litmus test of this process that it enables and promotes the participation of especially disadvantaged groups such as older people. Such participation of older people is also desirable in terms of their potentially significant contribution of knowledge and expertise. However, experience indicates that the views of older people, unless they are in positions of influence and prestige, rarely gain a hearing.

Over time, however, the adjustment of development strategies to take account of the involvement of increasing numbers of older people will not be an option but a necessity. In the same way that an issue like that of the conservation of the environment has, in the course of two decades, moved from the fringe to the centre of the development debate, questions raised by demographic changes will become increasingly difficult to ignore. However, it is unlikely to be easy to break down the barriers of prejudice which militate against the right of older people, in common with the rest of the population, both 'to have more and to be more' through the process of development. For any society,

It is ... the entire system of values that define the meaning and value of old age. The reverse applies: by the way in which a society behaves towards its old people it uncovers the naked, and often carefully hidden, truth about its real principles and aims. (de Beauvoir, 1972)

Notes

1 'Population ageing' refers to the increasing proportion of older people within a population.
2 Chronological age has many limitations in defining 'ageing', given the wide range of factors which affect the ageing process. However, it continues to be widely used, and is adopted here for convenience. The UN World Assembly on Ageing in 1982 focused on people aged 60 years or more as its main concern, and this is the threshold age used here, unless otherwise stated.
3 The term 'handicap', as used in the study quoted here, has a precise technical definition, distinguishing it from disability and impairment.

References

Andrews, G.R. et al., 1985, *Ageing in the Western Pacific*, Manila: World Health Organisation.

de Beauvoir, S., 1972, *Old Age*, London: Andre Deutsch, Weidenfeld & Nicholson.

Cattell, M.G., 1990, 'Models of old age among the Samia of Kenya', *Journal of Cross-Cultural Gerontology* 5:4.

Coles, C., 1991, 'Hausa women's work in a declining urban economy' in C. Coles and B. Mack, *Hausa Women in the Twentieth Century*, Madison: University of Wisconsin Press.

Cowgill, D.O., 1986, *Aging Around the World*, Belmont, Ca.: Wadsworth.

Dowd, J.E. and K.G. Manton, 1992, 'Projections of disability consequences in Indonesia', *Journal of Cross-Cultural Gerontology* 7:3.

Goldstein, M.C., S. Schuler, and J.L. Ross, 1983, 'Social and economic forces affecting intergenerational relations in extended families in a Third World country: a cautionary tale from South Asia', *Journal of Gerontology* 38:6.

HelpAge International, 1993a, 'Improving the Situation of Elderly People in the Marginal Areas of North Lima', unpublished project report.

HelpAge International, 1993b, 'The Situation of Older Refugees from Burundi in Tanzania', unpublished report.

HelpAge International, 1993c, unpublished tour report.

Ingstad B. et al, 1992, 'Care for the elderly, care by the elderly: the role of elderly women in a changing Tswana society', *Journal of Cross-Cultural Gerontology* 7:4.

Jacquemin J., 1993, 'Elderly Women and the Family', paper presented at the NGO Forum to launch UN International Year of the Family, Malta.

Jazdowska N., 1992, 'Elderly Women Caring for Orphans and People with AIDS', unpublished survey report for HelpAge Zimbabwe.

Kalache, A., 1991, 'Ageing in developing countries' in M.J. Pathy (ed.): *Principles and Practice of Geriatric Medicine*, London: John Wiley and Sons.

Kaur, M. *et al.*, 1987, 'Socio-economic profile of the rural aged' in Sharma and Dak (eds.).

Kinsella, K. and C.M. Taeuber, 1993, *An Aging World II*, Washington DC: US Bureau of the Census International Population Reports.

Liu, L., 1982, 'Mandatory retirement and other reforms pose new challenges for China's government', *Aging and Work* 5:2.

Martin, L.G., 1990, 'The status of South Asia's growing elderly population', *Journal of Cross-Cultural Gerontology* 5:2.

Neysmith, S.M. and J. Edwardh, 1984, 'Economic dependency in the 1980s: its impact on Third World elderly', *Ageing and Society* 4:1.

Pratt, B. and J. Boyden, 1985, *The Field Directors' Handbook*, Oxford: Oxfam.

Rosenmayr, L., 1991, 'Health of rural elderly in Mali', *Journal of Cross-Cultural Gerontology* 6:3.

Schulz, J.H., 1991, *The World Ageing Situation*, New York: United Nations.

Sen, K., 1993, *Ageing, Health, Social Change and Policy in Developing Countries*, London: London School of Hygiene and Tropical Medicine.

Sennott-Miller, L., 1989, 'The health and socioeconomic situation of midlife and older women in Latin America and the Caribbean', *Mid-Life and Older Women in Latin America and the Caribbean*, Washington DC: PAHO/AARP.

Sharma, M.L. and T.M. Dak (eds.), 1987, *Ageing in India*, Delhi: Ajanta Publications.

Sokolovsky, J., 1991, 'Introduction to special section on health, aging and development', *Journal of Cross-Cultural Gerontology* 6:3.

Tout, K., 1989, *Ageing in Developing Countries*, Oxford: Oxford University Press.

The author

Mark Gorman is Deputy Chief Executive at HelpAge International. This article first appeared in *Development in Practice*, Volume 5, Number 2, in 1995.

Culture, liberation, and 'development'

Shubi L. Ishemo

Introduction

It has become a fetish to talk about traditions when referring to socio-economic processes in Africa. This is common not only among Western 'development experts', but also among some African intellectuals. 'Tradition' carries with it meanings of timelessness, of stasis, of being fossilised. For the society so described, the notion of 'tradition' denies it a history. The implications for such an approach are manifest in the economistic ideology of 'developmentalism', which, as Shivji (1986:1) has shown, has been 'the dominant ideological formation in post-independence Africa'. The basis for this ideology, he further notes, is as follows:

We are economically backward and we need to develop and develop very fast. In this task of development we cannot afford the luxury of politics. Therefore politics are relegated to the background, while economics come to occupy the central place on the ideological terrain.

We might also add that, in this ideological formation, culture, like politics, is seen as an obstacle and therefore relegated to the background. This obsession with economistic developmentalism is not new. It has historically, and in various forms, served to legitimate domination over working people in every society. Historically, too, in the relationship between the West and the South, it has been based on the belief that the processes of Western socio-economic and political development are universal and that

these, and these alone, constitute progress. It has been the dominant view since the age of European 'Enlightenment' in the eighteenth century and was popularised during colonial times. It has, in various guises, dominated the policies not only of the Western 'donor' governments, some NGOs, and international financial institutions, but also of some Southern governments. That dominant view is Eurocentric, in that it assumes that the Western model is superior. It carries with it biases and lack of concern for the cultures and history of African and other Southern societies.

National liberation as an 'act of culture'

It is important to remind ourselves of the historical dimension. Colonialism, in Africa in particular and the South in general, served the need of the highly industrialised countries in Europe and North America for capital accumulation. In spite of political independence, this has not changed; in fact it has been consolidated, as capital restructures itself to resolve the crisis and to ensure continued accumulation through a variety of mechanisms. I shall come to this later. The colonialists started from the premise that Africa had no history; their mission was to bring the continent into history. Those ideas therefore denied Africa a culture and served as an ideological licensing of exploitation.

In the struggle for national liberation, the

issue of history and culture became central. Amilcar Cabral, a revolutionary theorist and leader of the PAIGC liberation movement in Guinea-Bissau and Cabo Verde, wrote:

Our countries are economically backward. Our peoples are at a specific historical stage, characterized by this backward condition of our economy. We must be conscious of this. We are African peoples, we have not invented many things ... we have no big factories ... but we do have our own hearts, our own heads and our own history. It is this history which the colonialists have taken from us. The colonialists usually say that it is they who brought us into history: today we say that this is not so. They made us leave history, our history, to follow them, right at the back, to follow the progress of their history.

Cabral argued that the national liberation struggle was a way 'to return to our history, on our own feet, by our own means and through our own sacrifices' (1974:63). Imperialist and colonial domination was therefore 'the negation of the historical process of the dominated people by means of violently usurping the free operation of the process of development of the productive forces' (1973:41). By 'productive forces', Cabral meant the means of production (such as tools, premises, instrumental materials and raw materials) and labour power. He emphasised that every society is an 'evolving entity', and that the stage of its development can be seen in the level of its productive forces. Each of these reacts to nature. Groups enter material relationships, relationships with nature and the environment, and relationships among individuals or collectives. To him, these components constitute not only history, but also culture. In usurping all these, imperialism practises cultural oppression. Therefore, national liberation aims at the 'liberation of the process of development of national productive forces' and consequently the ability to determine the mode of production most appropriate to the evolution of the liberated people. It necessarily opens up new prospects for the cultural development of the

society in question, by returning to that society all its capacity to create progress. National liberation, therefore, is 'necessarily an act of culture' (1973:43).

Cabral warned (1973:52) against naturalising culture and linking it to supposed racial characteristics.

It is important to be conscious of the value of African culture in the framework of universal civilisation, but to compare this value with that of other cultures, not with a view of deciding its superiority or inferiority, but in order to determine, in the general framework of the struggle for progress, what contribution African culture has made and can make, and what are the contributions it can or must receive from elsewhere.

Cabral saw culture as a 'fruit of history', an integral part of historical processes. The most fundamental element for progress was the regaining of people's creative capacity and potential, which imperialism had usurped. This creative capacity has a democratic content, in that people determine what is best for themselves, and adapt new techniques and knowledge to their concrete reality. So when we speak about culture, we are referring not just to customs, beliefs, attitudes, values, art, etc., but to the whole way of life of a people, which also embraces a complex web of economic and political activities, science, and technology. These are not exclusive attributes of any single race or people. He referred to a scientific culture, a universal culture free from domination (1973:55).

I have dwelt on Cabral's work at length, because his analysis of the positive role of culture is relevant in the struggle against the most pressing problems of our time. His profound work has been shamefully ignored, especially by those in positions to exert a positive influence on policy and strategies that meet the needs and interests of the working people.

'Development' policies and cultural dependency

Much of the debate about 'development' has been conducted from differing and contending perspectives. It is not my intention to consider that here, but I wish to dwell briefly on how some of these perspectives have dealt with the cultural dimension in 'development' policies.

Modernisation theories regard cultures of non-industrialised societies in the South as obstacles to development. Those societies are seen as being characterised by kinship (which apparently hinders individual enterprise), religious obscurantism and fatalism, stagnation and resignation. In short, they are 'traditional'. The opposite of this is a 'modern' capitalist sector.

From a different source, another perspective, associated with Warren (1980), sees underdevelopment as being internal to poor societies of the South, and argues for a 'progressive' mission of capitalist imperialism. With specific reference to Africa, this position is unrelentingly restated in the words of John Sender and Sheila Smith (1987). They see capitalist imperialism as having led to the development of the productive forces and a rise in living standards. Both perspectives share the super-ficial nature of the dichotomy between tradition and modernity; both dwell purely on economic factors, and see the causes of the crisis in Africa as internal.

Recently, as Samir Amin (1990:96) has pointed out, the cultural dimension has been embraced by researchers as an important element in socio-economic processes. To my mind, however, this is not new. For working people in poor countries of the South, it has always been at the heart of any initiative that affects their lives. Central to the cultural dimension of socio-economic processes is the question of identity. Samir Amin further draws contrasts between the development of capitalism in Western Europe and Japan, on the one hand, and in Africa on the other. In the former he sees a longer process of social transformation with 'no break but a complex

process of selective repossession of former cultural components within the context of technological and economic development'. This explains the dynamism of economic and technological creativity of those societies. By contrast, capitalist development in Africa was imposed from the outside and confronted local cultures in a violent manner, with the result that 'Identity ..., rather than being gradually broken down and rebuilt to productive effect, is more or less ferociously destroyed, without putting in place compensatory processes of production of new cultural components, capable in turn of supporting accumulation and innovation' (1990: 98-9).

The origins of Africa's problems lie in the specificity of capitalist development and its long-term effects on African societies. It is fair to state that the European model was forced down their throats. African people had no say in this, because that was the nature of the Eurocentric project. It precluded all positive knowledge that African societies had generated.

Colonial institutions inculcated Eurocentric values unremittingly. European intellectuals served to legitimate the Eurocentric project. As George Joseph (1990:3) and his colleagues have argued,

During the heyday of imperialism, the scholar was useful, not only in constructing a conceptual framework within which colonial ideology could be defended and extended, but in helping to select problems for investigation which highlighted the beneficial effects of colonial rule.

The purpose of colonial research institutes like the Rhodes-Livingstone Institute in the then Northern Rhodesia (now Zambia) is too well known to repeat here. In many colonies, ethnicities were invented; in the case of post-colonial Rwanda and Burundi, the cumulative consequences of the invention of ethnic identities by the successive German and Belgian colonial administrations are all too painfully apparent. The study of African cultures served the needs of colonial occupiers, particularly in the creation of labour reservoirs and the segmentation of labour along ethnic lines. It was not meant to invigorate and energise those societies to absorb and adapt new positive elements to their own realities. This was reinforced by the colonial education system. African intellectuals were colonised. The medium of instruction became European languages, whose cultural influences cannot be underestimated. Cultural dependency has been the consequence of that process.

It is in this context that socio-economic, political, cultural, and intellectual processes in post-colonial Africa must be understood. The penetrating analysis of Amilcar Cabral of the role of culture in the processes of change is very relevant, not only in contemporary Africa, but also throughout the South. He made a distinction between

the situation of the masses, who preserve their culture, and that of the social groups who are assimilated or partially so, who are cut off and culturally alienated. Even though the indigenous colonial elite who emerged during the process of colonization still continue to pass on some element of indigenous culture, yet they live both materially and spiritually according to the foreign culture. They seek to identify themselves increasingly with this culture both in their social behaviours and even in their appreciation of its values. (1973:61)

In identifying the latter group, Cabral made a further distinction between those who vacillated and those who identified themselves with the masses. Post-colonial Africa has by and large been dominated by the vacillators. They have collaborated with imperialism in determining the strategies for 'development', by failing to challenge models that do not address people's needs. Their strategies reflect an unthinking and uncritical imitation of the West. They are intellectual and cultural captives of imperialism. This is not to say that this model has not been challenged in post-colonial Africa. Some of the liberation movements were a source of

great inspiration for many. There were, in those movements, some 'organic' intellectuals like Amilcar Cabral who studied the reality of their societies meticulously. From such study they identified themselves with the aspirations of the masses and created popular structures in which the people participated in devising strategies for economic, social, political, and cultural advancement. In some countries, progressive strategies, designed to meet the people's needs, were initiated — even if sometimes frustrated by a lack of clear reference to the cultural dimension, by bureaucratism, and by populism. 'Organic' or politically engaged intellectuals played an important part in opening up avenues for real advancement. (There are some excellent essays on this subject in Diouf and Mamdani, eds., 1994.) We know what happened to those strategies and those intellectuals. External intervention and local reaction stifled them and continue to frustrate them.

Corporate profits and the quality of life

The current structural adjustment policies (SAPs), though they have their origins in the period dating from the early 1980s, are not new. What is new is the bold and shameless assertion of their neo-liberal ideological underpinnings and the intensity and viciousness of their implementation. SAPs have had devastating effects on the living standards of working people, including unprecedented increases in the levels of unemployment and a decline in levels of pay. Emphasis on export-led commodity production to service an ever-increasing debt to the international financial institutions (IFIs) has resulted in low productive capacity for the internal market and an increase in dependency on (often subsidised) Western agro-industrial conglomerates. As Samir Amin (1994:38) has noted, IFIs like the World Bank have 'focused on destroying the autonomy of the peasant world, breaking the subsistence economy by supporting forms of credit designed to this end, and promoting the differentiation of the rural world through the famous "green revolution"'. The conditionalities imposed by the IFIs have led to a decrease in social expenditure and the deterioration of health-care and education systems (Chossudovsky, 1991 and Committee for Academic Freedom in Africa, 1992). Many studies show a correlation between debt, SAPs, and ecological deterioration. For the World Bank, pollution is a sign of progress. In a famous observation, Lawrence Summers, the Bank's vice-president, recommended the transfer of 'dirty' industries to the Third World:

I think the economic logic behind dumping a load of toxic waste in the lowest wage country is impeccable and we should face up to that ... I have always thought that under-populated countries in Africa are vastly under-polluted, their air quality is probably vastly inefficiently high compared to Los Angeles or Mexico City. (Dore, 1992:85)

It is clear that, as Samir Amin (1994:38) has argued, 'The Bank has never seen itself as a "public institution" competing or potentially clashing with private capital (transnationals). On the contrary, it has viewed itself as an agent whose task is to support their penetration of the Third World.' The SAPs are economistic. They are more concerned with corporate profits than enabling the working people to improve the quality of their lives. In ignoring environmental issues, they downplay the cultural dimension; for, as Cabral (1973:42) noted, when we speak of culture, we refer to 'relationships between (humanity) and nature, between (humanity) and his (her) environment'. Thus, as Dore (1992:84) has observed, it is not surprising that, in the Third World, contemporary struggles of the working people have reflected the 'fusion of ecological, economic and cultural struggles'.

SAPs have engendered a culture of unbridled consumerism, with sections of the cities bristling with luxury commodities which are well beyond the means of working people. Far from inaugurating a new epoch of progress, they have exacerbated inequalities and weakened social bonds and solidarity through emphasis on the individual, rather than on society or communities.

Under empty slogans of a compressed world and a globalised economy, the sovereignty of the fragile nation states has been weakened. Decisions that affect millions are made in the boardrooms of the IMF and the World Bank, fully supported by the Western governments. 'Democracy' is imposed and regulated from the outside. The fall of authoritarian regimes has been a welcome development, but the popular content of that change has been hijacked by those committed to the neo-liberal project. The implications for people's participation in determining their strategies for advancement have been negative. Initiatives from below have been constantly frustrated by obsession with the laws of the market.

Acknowledging 'people as a living presence'

In 1979, Adrian Adams wrote an excellent account of a peasant co-operative in Senegal. It is one of the most moving and inspiring accounts that I have ever read. There is every reason to believe that there have been and continue to be similar experiences throughout the South. It is necessary reading for anyone who is serious about real 'development'. Adams details the development of a peasant farmers' initiative to improve their food production and to 'base rural development on existing communities and values'. The peasants' appeal for help to Western NGOs to adapt irrigation technical inputs to their farming methods attracted an array of NGOs, the Senegalese State bureaucracy, and USAID, all vying to control and direct what the peasants had initiated. What emerged was a predetermined Eurocentric approach, which ignored the peasants and brushed them aside as ignorant of 'development'. Technical 'assistance' was conditional on the peasants dismantling collective forms of production and parcelling out land into individual family plots, growing rice instead of millet, having production targets imposed on them by the State, purchasing fertilisers beyond their needs, and virtually surrendering control of their bank accounts to the State. The peasants rejected this paternalism, clearly recognising the peril that has befallen many poor countries: '*You go into debt, and then you have to sell them your whole harvest to pay off your debt. We don't want debts. We just want freedom*' (Adams 1979:458). The people wanted 'peasant development' with '*a common fund, to give us strength. We, ourselves, decide what we want to do. We, ourselves, decide how many hectares we want to plant. We are working for our own people*' (p.463).

They rejected top-down 'administrative development'. The issue then was: what constitutes 'development'? Those so-called 'experts', as Adams correctly noted, were unable to 'acknowledge the existence of a people here and now, having a past and a future' or 'to acknowledge the people as a living presence'. Indeed, that 'living presence' is the culture of a people.

What emerges from Adams' account of the struggle of the people in one Senegalese village is the sheer arrogance on the part of the self-appointed 'aid experts', compounded by the complicity of the State bureaucracy. Such arrogance in some 'donors', some political leaders and bureaucrats, transnational corporations and their local agents has been pervasive throughout the South. A catalogue of misconceived projects would be of biblical length. Those who initiate major infra-structural projects — dams, for example — neither consult the local population nor take into account their way of life, which includes, above all, accumulated knowledge of the ecological balance, their beliefs, and their sacred sites. This amounts to what Saleth (1992) has termed 'bypassing and alienating economic development', which reinforces existing inequalities of access to land and the displacement of the most vulnerable sections of the peasantry. Examples of these, and the opposition they have generated, can be found in India, where there has been a courageous struggle by peasants to halt a dam project sponsored by the World Bank and supported by the Indian Government; or in Namibia, where a government-proposed dam project which would have long-term effects on the Himba pastoral people has created controversy and led some officials into scathing condemnation of those who defend 'bare breasted' and 'primitive' people (*The Observer*, 29 January 1995) standing in the way of modernisation. And recently the activities of Michelin, the giant Western rubber conglomerate operating in Nigeria, have similarly shown the top-down approach to 'development'. There, the company expanded a rubber plantation into the protected Okomu forest without concern for the environment and the culture of the local people. It destroyed medicinal trees, shrines, and other symbols dear to the beliefs of the inhabitants. In reply to protests, the company pleaded ignorance and added, 'But we know the impact on the community can only be positive. We are providing employment, schools, clinics, electricity and water supplies' (*Financial Times*, 8 March 1995).

Of course, no local inhabitant objects to schools or clinics. But the company has a different conception of 'development', which involves destroying the symbols of the people's identity. The company, probably with the complicity of State bureaucrats, does not involve the local people in decision-making or incorporate their world-view into projects.

Some NGOs operate on the same basis. The case of their operations in Mozambique is well documented in Joe Hanlon's study (1991). A number of African academics (such as Ayesha Imam and Amina Mama, 1994, and Abdel Gadir Ali, 1994) have noted that some NGOs and other 'donors' deliberately ignore locally funded research and wheel in 'experts' (from Europe and North America) whose recommendations carry more weight than the work of the local intelligentsia. In an example from Sudan, Abdel Gadir Ali (1994) notes how the Sudanese economists who were critical of structural adjustment policies were deliberately excluded from an ILO mission requested by the Sudanese government to study the economic situation and advise on long-term strategies. Ali (1994:112) details the ensuing struggle which the local intelligentsia waged, and how 'a donor community with substantial resources waging a media war on local research efforts expressing reservations on the results of an established donor community's wisdom on how an African economy should be managed'. Consequently, as Mama and Imam (1994:86) have noted, African intellectuals are 'forced to take on board [Eurocentric] norms and waste time tilting at windmills to find out why we deviate from these patterns, instead of finding out what our own patterns and realities are'.

Making cultural sense of technology

Technology which is imposed on the people can be ill-suited to local needs. Bina Agarwal's study (1986:79-80) of wood-fuel crisis in the South shows how new cooking-stove technology, designed to save wood fuel, ended by doing exactly the opposite. In Guatemala, one important function of the 'traditional' stove was to emit smoke, which killed mosquitoes and pests in corn ears hung from rafters. This benefit was lost when the new stoves were introduced. When a new stove was introduced in Ghana, women found it technically cumbersome and ill-suited to using many pots at once. Local artisans and women had not been consulted in the design of the stoves. These projects claimed to employ 'appropriate technology', but they wholly failed to consider local needs and cultures. They assumed peasants in their ignorance to be responsible for the depletion of wood fuel, and presumed to import European science and technology to resolve their problems. As a consequence of not being

consulted and involved in the development of new techniques, local artisans have become de-skilled. Such technologies are useless, because they are not specific to local techniques and they are not culturally familiar. The starting point for the introduction of new technology must be to recognise, as Vandana Shiva (1991) has noted, that all societies have 'ways of knowing' and 'ways of doing' and that

all societies, in all their diversity, have had science and technology systems on which their distinct and diverse development have been based. Technologies or systems of technologies bridge the gap between nature's resources and human needs. Systems of knowledge and culture provide the framework for the perception and utilisation of natural resources.

Technology is therefore not culture-free. It is central to the question of identity. Since it constitutes 'ways of doing', it is one of the principal elements of a people's identity. You can have science and technology, but with no 'development'. The two must make cultural sense, to achieve true development. In their campaign to establish a just international economic order, non-industrialised countries, through the South Commission [1990:45-46, 80, 132], chaired by former Tanzanian president Julius Nyerere, strongly argued for the centrality of culture in economic processes:

Capital formation and technical progress are essential elements of development, but the broad environment for their effectiveness is a society's culture; it is only by the affirmation and enrichment of cultural identities through mass participation that development can be given strong roots and made a sustained process. For only on secure cultural foundations can a society maintain its cohesion and security during the profound changes that are the concomitants of development and economic modernisation.

The Commission recommended that strategies must be sensitive to cultural roots, that is values, attitudes, and beliefs, and that cultural advancement itself depends on people-centred strategies. It warned that strategies which ignore the cultural dimen-sion could result in indifference, alienation, social discord, and obscurantist responses.

These warnings have not been heeded. As I have noted above, economistic approaches that are central to the neo-liberal agenda have unleashed social instability. Ethnic rivalries and religious fundamentalism are a consequence of a profound sense of deprivation unleashed by 'structural adjust-ment'. As Samir Amin (1990:98) has argued, 'fundamentalism emerged as a cultural protest against economics', and 'its growth [is] largely conditioned by the forms of social and economic change'.

The obstinate reluctance of the donors and Western governments to understand the atomising tendencies of 'structural adjust-ment' is mirrored in new concepts such as 'global culture'. These are based on the restructuring of capital on a global scale; the proliferation of consumerism, propagated by new communication technologies; and the supposed irrelevance of national frontiers. Western governments, transnationals, and their intellectual underlings harp on 'globalisation' without asking who gains and who loses (in economic, political, and cultural terms). 'Global culture' is a Western construct (particularly dear to the Western media). It is a piece of ideological baggage designed to legitimate 'structural adjustment'. It is an expression of cultural imperialism which particularly affects young people in poor countries.

Cultural penetration is linked to economic exploitation and ultimately to political and military domination. During the late 1970s and early 1980s, Third World countries waged a struggle within the framework of UNESCO to establish a New World Com-munication and Information Order. The principal issue of the debate was the ever-increasing unidirectional flow of cultural products and 'news' from the advanced capitalist countries to the South, and the distorting effect on the cultures of Southern societies. The West condemned the Third World moves as politically motivated, claiming that they amounted to an infringe-ment of the freedom of information. The United States and Britain withdrew from UNESCO in protest. It is clear that the monopoly over the news media and the distribution of cultural products was linked to the Western monopoly over information and communication technology. Third World attempts to link culture to the wider issue of a more just world economic order led to the West's campaign to weaken UN structures. These had been effective channels in a collective struggle for a more just inter-national order. Their replacement, through the strong-arm tactics of the Western govern-ments and the transnationals, by the 'unholy trinity' of the IMF, World Bank, and the World Trade Organisation has implications of an economic, political and culture nature for Africa and the rest of the South. It amounts to recolonisation.

Traditional cultures and knowledge have also attracted attention from the pharma-ceutical and cosmetics transnationals. Some are well known for operating under hollow slogans of 'fair trade' and 'empowerment' of poor peoples. At the same time, the West demands 'rights' of intellectual property over Southern flora, fauna, and (increasingly) human achievement.

This is the civilisation, the globalisation, the 'development' that apparently will bestow benefits of the 'market' on working people in Africa, Asia, and Latin America! That there has been a peasant uprising in Chiapas is not surprising. If more rebellions break out, they will, under the circumstances, be justified. Maybe NGOs should look carefully at whose side they are on.

References

Adams, A., 1979, 'An open letter to a young researcher', *African Affairs* 78: 451-79.
Agarwal, B., 1986, *Cold Hearths and Barren*

Slopes, The Woodfuel Crisis in the Third World, London: Zed.

Ali, A. G., 1994, 'Donors' wisdom versus African folly: what academic freedom and which high moral standing?' in M. Diouf and M. Mamdani (eds), 1994.

Amin, S., 1990, *Maldevelopment. Anatomy of a Global Failure*, London: Zed.

Amin, S., 1994, 'Fifty years is enough', *Southern African Economics and Political Monthly*, November.

Cabral, A., 1973, *Return to the Source*, New York: Africa Information Service.

Cabral, A., 1974, *Revolution in Guinea, An African People's Struggle*, London: Stage 1.

Chossudovsky, M., 1991, 'Global poverty and new world economic order', *Economic and Political Weekly*, 2 November.

Committee for Academic Freedom in Africa, 1992, 'The World Bank and education in Africa', *Race and Class* 34/1.

Diouf, M. and M. Mamdani (eds.), 1994, *Academic Freedom in Africa*, Dakar: CODESRIA.

Dore, E., 1992, 'Debt and ecological disaster in Latin America', *Race and Class* 34/1.

Hanlon, J., 1991, *Mozambique: Who Calls the Shots?*, London: James Currey.

Imam, A. M., 1994, 'The role of academics in limiting and expanding academic freedom', in Diouf and Mamdani (eds.) 1994.

Joseph, G., V. Reddy, and M. Searle-Chatterjee, 1990, 'Eurocentrism in the social sciences', *Race and Class* 31/4.

Saleth, R. M., 1992, 'Big dams controversy: economics, ecology and equity', *Economic and Political Weekly*, 25 July.

Sender, J. and S. Smith, 1987, *The Development of Capitalism in Africa*, London: Methuen.

Shiva, V., 1991, 'Biotechnology development and conservation of biodiversity', *Economic and Political Weekly*, 30 Nov.

Shivji, I. G., 1986, *The State and the Working People in Tanzania*, Dakar: CODESRIA.

The South Commission, 1990, *The Challenge to the South*, Oxford: Oxford University Press.

Warren, Bill, 1980, *Imperialism: Pioneer of Capital*, London: Verso.

The author

Shubi L. Ishemo is a Tanzanian historian teaching at Trinity and All Saints, University of Leeds. His latest book, *The Lower Zambezi Basin in Mozambique, 1850-1920: A study in economy and society*, was published by Avebury in 1995.

This article first appeared in *Development in Practice* Volume 5, Number 3, in 1995.

The politics of development in longhouse communities in Sarawak, East Malaysia

Dimbab Ngidang

Introduction

A variety of intervention strategies have been used to improve the standard of living of Sarawak's rural population. They range from rural health services provided by the Medical Department, and adult education conducted by the Department of Community Development (KEMAS), to 'intensive' extension programmes implemented by the Department of Agriculture, and integrated agricultural development projects promoted under the National Agricultural Policy.

Although most people believe that government intervention makes a critical contribution to assisting the rural poor, not everyone agrees on how it should be carried out. In government-sponsored projects, extension agents can find themselves expected to act as political agents, while a participatory approach is seldom used in rural development programmes.

This article discusses the role of communication in government interventions to promote agricultural projects among the Dayak longhouse communities in Sarawak. (The term 'longhouse' refers to wooden houses, linked together in a single row: the typical dwelling place of Dayak tribes in Sarawak. Dayak communities consist of several tribal groups: Iban, Bidayuh, Kayan, Kenyah, Murut, Kelabit, and Penan. In this article the term 'longhouse communities' is used interchangeably with 'Dayak communities'.)

Rationale for intervention

There is a limit to what poor people can do with the resources at their disposal. Without government aid, it is impossible for the poor to overcome the constraints imposed by lack of financial and material resources. If the doctrine of self-help is imposed on them and taken too far, the notion of self-reliance could work against the interests of the poor. Furthermore, providing no outside inputs whatsoever, in order to avoid the dangers of paternalism and the spurious authority of 'outside experts', could do more harm than good. According to Khan (1975), priming the pump to trigger local initiatives may enable top-down initiatives to promote bottom-up impetus for development.

Despite the government's good intentions, development efforts in Sarawak are often complicated by political conflicts and structural rigidities imposed by prevailing socio-economic and political systems. This article explains how government-initiated development programmes are usually characterised by 'centre-periphery biases' (Chambers, 1983:76).

Development handouts

One major challenge facing the Sarawak State government, since independence was gained through the formation of Malaysia in 1963, is eradicating rural poverty, and improving the standard of living by modernising the agricultural sector (King, 1987 and 1988). In the past three decades, agricultural extension programmes have been used to reach out to the farming communities; they constitute the first major step in bringing about socio-economic transformation in the rural areas (Cramb, 1988).[1] A major goal of these extension programmes in Sarawak is to 'domesticate' the so-called shifting cultivators: mainly Dayak rural dwellers, whose livelihood depends on hill rice farming.

Subsidy schemes — the planting of rubber, pepper, cocoa, and oil palm on a commercial basis to encourage cash cropping — have been extensively employed as a tool for persuading the Dayak communities to abandon subsistence agriculture. In the late 1970s, these development 'handouts', or production incentives, funded by the World Bank, were packaged with 'training-and-visit' extension services.

Incentives often constitute an important policy instrument for achieving development goals. However, since agricultural inputs have now been given to farmers as free 'gifts', these material incentives have their shortcomings. In particular, a 'subsidy syndrome' has become widespread in rural areas of Sarawak. Handouts have created dependency among farmers: because they have no obligation to repay the government, they have little commitment to government-sponsored projects, nor do they attach a socio-economic value to the 'incentives'.[2]

In addition, offering assistance to farmers as an inducement to plant cash crops and adopt new farm technology can be counter-productive and open to abuse. Free inputs can be sold for quick cash: in other words, the resources required for improving productivity can be sold for short-term benefits.

Development assistance cannot be evaluated separately from the political purpose of rural development. There are two interpretations of this. Firstly, getting subsidies from the government indicates that rural people have some political leverage. This implies that bottom-up demand leads to top-down responses from the government. Secondly, since agricultural inputs are important resources, supplying them will enable State officials to exercise some control over them. This is commonplace, whether in developing or developed countries, as far as subsidies are concerned: development is invariably political.

Maintaining the cycle of poverty

It is a common belief that if the longhouse communities abandon subsistence farming and pursue cash cropping — planting of pepper, cocoa, oil palm, and rubber — their farm productivity can be enhanced and so bring about capital accumulation and savings. This, in turn, is expected to enable farmers to attain a state of economic 'take-off', enabling them eventually to be self-reliant. It is argued that when farm productivity is increased, rural poverty will be eradicated. This seems an attractive theory, but the question remains: 'Can it be effectively applied?'

In the past 30 years, government-sponsored projects have produced mixed results. Government efforts have certainly had a positive impact on the adoption of cash cropping among longhouse communities and an improvement in crop production, but these efforts have not necessarily resulted in an increase in income, let alone in self-reliance.

Three major forces have been identified as responsible for maintaining the *status quo*. Firstly, the external factor: world-markets do not take individuals or theories of development into consideration. Farmers are constantly affected by the fluctuation in prices of agricultural commodities, which are indeed vulnerable to changes in supply and demand on the world market.

Secondly, there are internal factors, of which there are two main categories: those pertaining to the environmental ecosystem and those resulting from structural variables. An environmental ecosystem refers to the risks and uncertainties brought about by diseases, pests, and climatic factors, all of which are beyond the farmer's control.[3]

The second category of internal forces which perpetuates a vicious circle of poverty among longhouse communities are structural variables, which encompass an interplay of socio-cultural and political factors. For instance, longhouse communities are affected not only by world markets, but also by internal markets, destabilised by the manipulative activities of well-established networks of middlemen. Since farmers' organisations are still in their infancy, most agricultural products are marketed by individual farmers themselves.

Dandot (1987) pointed out that one of the most critical internal constraints on agricultural development is associated with a complex land-classification and land-tenure system — Native Customary Rights (NCR) Land.[4] As an editorial in the journal of the Society of Progress (*Journal AZAM*) expressed it in August 1987, 'Land is plentiful', but 'it is not always readily available for development. This is particularly the case with NCR land.' There is no doubt that unproductive use of Native Customary Rights Land among Dayak communities constitutes a major poverty-related problem. Despite official assurance, many longhouse communities are still sceptical about government policy concerning the design of land-development projects.

Most rural areas of Sarawak are served by insufficient roads and poor transport facilities. As a result, access to markets is very limited, and only those living in the vicinity of urban centres are able to benefit from infrastructural facilities provided by the government.

Another problem is farmers' lack of access to institutional credit, explained by their disadvantaged socio-economic position, which has caused them to rely primarily on production credit provided by the local Chinese traders, or 'towkays'. More often than not, they end up in debt after paying exorbitant rates of interest.

High rates of illiteracy and the apparent lack of motivation for pursuing higher education are two of the factors which impede rapid progress among longhouse communities, as compared with the Malay and Chinese communities in

Sarawak. This has caused the longhouse communities to be excluded from mainstream socio-economic development in Sarawak.

Perhaps the most important factor working against the integration of longhouse communities is political conflict among Dayak leaders. Problems arise because the leaders are often affiliated to different political parties. There is always a tendency for different political orientations to create animosity and factionalism,[5] which impede any development efforts.

Cash-generating projects are only a partial solution to eradicating poverty, since people are not developed through agriculture alone. The government's current strategy of agricultural development is just an interim measure to assist the very poorest of the poor.

A more feasible and logical approach to the development of longhouse communities is to educate the younger generation. Upward social mobility for longhouse dwellers is virtually impossible without a higher education. In other words, the critical issue is the long-term development of human resources through formal training, so that young people can join the mainstream professions and have the opportunity to become managers, technicians, and professionals.

Thirdly, the purpose of government-assisted self-help has certain internal contradictions. The original goal of subsidy schemes was to promote the cultivation of cash crops on a trial basis. The schemes are not intended to supply all the farm production inputs required by farmers. However, the distribution of these subsidies has also created a social dilemma. Not only has it created the 'subsidy syndrome', but, should these subsidies be disbanded, it may also jeopardise the political survival of some politicians.

Extension agents or government agents?

Extension agents play three important roles in promoting cash cropping among longhouse communities in Sarawak. These are:

- transferring new technology to farmers;
- organising farmers involved in agricultural projects;
- linking farmers to government agencies, through which they can gain access to services and resources, information and farm technology.[6]

In recent years, extension agents' linking roles have been re-defined to include public relations: they are expected to promote the government's political policies. According to Havelock's (1971) definition, the principal goal of such 'brokers' or intermediaries is to condition the attitudes and behaviour of longhouse communities and prepare them to participate actively in government-sponsored projects. The manner in which these agents operate is discussed in the next section.

There is a major problem inherent in this 'brokerage' role in rural development. While extension agents may have farmers' interests at heart, it is difficult for them to portray themselves as being independent of government interests, and to avoid extending the bureaucratic control imposed by government agencies. It is not customary for government agents to perform the empowering role that most advocates of participatory development would like to see in rural development. In addition, political elites usually seek some measure of social control over the process and the agents of development. Thus, the only way for rural populations to be free of external influence is to rely on their own resources.

People must make a choice: either accept government funding or pursue 'self-help' development. So far, no developing country can prove that progress can be achieved only through 'self-help'. In fact, 'self-help' development may even be detrimental to longhouse communities, because it removes the government's political obligation to assist the rural poor.

Village Development and Security Committees

One of the most important tasks of extension agents in Sarawak is to elicit cooperation from community leaders. The State authorities believe that a major hindrance to the successful implementation of development policies is resistance from leaders of longhouse communities. The official view is that, to bring about desirable socio-economic changes, the structure of traditional leadership must be changed and community leaders' views altered. In fact, it has long been recognised that it would be impossible to implement political policies without the participation of longhouse leaders.

Thus one way of winning support for government policies is to promote the participation of longhouse leadership in the administration of government-sponsored projects. For this reason, most rural development projects are implemented through a Village Development and Security Committee (VDSC) in an effort to organise longhouse communities.[7]

Specifically, there are four reasons for creating VDSCs:

- Extension agents are under official directives to work through VDSCs.

- Development programmes require legitimisation from local leadership prior to implementation.

- Eliciting community cooperation is easier when government agents are accepted by longhouse communities.

- A major assumption of grassroots development is that, if rural people can be brought into some form of organisational structure, their participation will be ensured. This leads to the common belief that rural people can organise themselves into action groups for articulating what they themselves perceive to be fundamental needs and interests.

In practice, the latter does not normally occur when organisers represent powerful outside interests. Local participation is imposed from the top. In West Malaysia, for example, VDSC members are mainly party sympathisers or cronies of local politicians and government appointees (Shamsul, 1989). The same applies to longhouse communities in Sarawak. Even though VDSC members are elected by the longhouse dwellers, the committee is not free from official control. This government-initiated committee is often designed as an appendage to the top-down system of development administration and coordination (Shamsul, op. cit.): an extension of government administrative machinery (Rauf, 1992), through which policies are implemented at a community level.

The roles of VDSCs in development programmes are prescribed by extension agents, following official top-down directives. This results in VDSC members playing two major roles in agricultural projects: persuading longhouse dwellers to implement officially-designed development plans, and organising activities for longhouse dwellers as required by extension agents' official plans.

VDSCs have very little political leverage to influence policy matters when major decisions are made beyond the boundaries of the longhouse authority. VDSC members lack organisational, technical, and managerial skills, because they are almost always illiterate. Development plans seldom incorp-orate capacity-building for VDSCs in exten-sion programmes. Occasionally, leadership training may be provided; however, it is mainly focused on the management of public relations.

This co-opted leadership can nevertheless be beneficial as well as problematic to the longhouse communities. One main advantage is that, when the longhouse leaders have made their commitment to support the government, their chances of obtaining development projects are very high. On the other hand, this may at times undermine a long-established solidarity among longhouse people.

Linkages through co-option

Extension agents acting as government agents, and VDSCs co-opted for political ends, demonstrate that development efforts are typically centred on patron-client relation-ships. There is the link between extension agent and VDSC, established under government directive, often with the specific motive of implementing the government's political policies in the form of development projects. And there is the link between VDSC and politicians: a primarily political linkage through which politicians draw support from local leadership.

Both kinds of link are established for promoting a mutual interdependence among extension agents, politicians, and VDSC members. The result is co-option: a process of absorbing VDSC members into leadership positions. This process facilitates the partici-pation of longhouse leaders in collective local decision-making processes. Also, it serves as a means through which politicians avert resistance or opposition to government policies from longhouse communities.

Politicians use such linkages to serve their individual private interests, by garnering support from longhouse communities in return for sponsoring development projects. Simultaneously, local politicians are under tremendous pressure to lobby for government projects in order to assist their constituencies. If they fail to reward their rural constituencies, their political survival may be at stake. Similarly, VDSCs may be rewarded with more political favours: promises of development when their political patrons get re-elected into office. Thus, these development projects serve as a powerful public-relations tool for the government.

Extension agents create these linkages to elicit cooperation from longhouse partners in the development of grassroots leadership; although, despite the government's efforts, very little progress has actually been achieved in this respect.[8]

While critics point out that this relationship can lead to resource-dependency among longhouse communities and may stifle community initiatives, it is unrealistic for resource-poor longhouse communities to reject government assistance. After all, VDSCs can use these links to obtain material resources, demand better services, and request agricultural projects from the government.

The politics of development

The government's intervention in rural development is explicitly stated in its policy of the 'politics of development'.[9] According to the Chief Minister of Sarawak (Mahmud, 1992:4), 'the politics of development is a total commitment to development by using the power of politics'. The policy demonstrates a far-reaching assumption about what politics can do, in either facilitating or hindering socio-economic and cultural development. From the standpoint of political stability, the Chief Minister of Sarawak justifies the 'politics of development' by claiming that it works for the good of rural beneficiaries. The policy has won widespread support among local media, NGOs, community leaders, and politicians.[10]

The 'politics of development' in Sarawak is intriguing, but not without a dilemma. Rewarding political allegiance is not unusual: every government does it. Longhouse communities which support government policy are rewarded with development projects, while those which oppose it are consigned to rely on self-help. It is commonplace, because it follows the principle of reciprocity: a simple logic of mutual interdependence among political affiliates.

However, this creates another problem — factionalism — which is a major obstacle facing government efforts in modernising the rural areas of Sarawak. One of the most important sources of factionalism derives from different political allegiances. Community conflicts are usually fuelled by the competing interests of local elites, representing different political parties in Sarawak.

Perhaps one of the greatest challenges facing the policy of 'politics of development' is that of

establishing a continuity of leadership. Many developing countries, although rich in natural resources, are still struggling to consolidate their efforts in rural development programmes. Part of the problem is due to poor leadership: there is no substitute for good political leadership in development.

Conclusions

Political intervention is a prerequisite to modernising socio-economic development in rural Sarawak. In the first place, there is no short-cut along the road to development. It is impossible to run away from controversies when development policies are directed to assisting different ethnic groups with diversified interests and political affiliations.

While a political intervention may sometimes provide short-term socio-economic gains, sustainable development is unachievable as long as longhouse dwellers remain illiterate. Progress depends on people themselves being developed.

However, development is basically the result of political choices: who gains and who loses depends very much upon the relative influence of particular groups in the process of decision-making (Leigh, 1988). When development policies are heavily top-down, subordination to political patronage is inevitable. But would it not be better to adopt a participatory approach, to elicit ideas, materials, and commitment from rural people in project planning and implementation, instead of relying exclusively on a conventional top-down strategy?

Acknowledgements

I am very grateful to Professors John Fett and Richard Powers, Department of Agricultural Journalism, Mr David Glendale, a PhD candidate of the Centre for Southeast Asian Studies, University of Wisconsin-Madison, and Mrs Eileen Marcus, Universiti Pertanian Malaysia Bintulu Campus, for their suggestions and comments on this paper.

Notes

1 As Melkote (1988:239) pointed out, 'agricultural extension has traditionally been regarded as the most logical, scientific, and systematic method of dis-seminating new knowledge and skills to farmers to aid them in successfully adopting innovations and making a more efficient use of their land and allied resources'.

2 See the *Sarawak Tribune*, 10 July 1993, p. 2, for an argument against financing full costs of Minor Rural Projects (MRPs).

3 See Ngidang *et al.* (1989:26) for a discussion of why farmers abandoned their pepper gardens.

4 The Land Code was introduced on 1 January 1958 (Hong, 1987; Colchester, 1991). The land law classifies all land in Sarawak into several categories (Foo and Lu, 1991). Privately owned land is classified as Mixed Zones. This category of land has document of title which can be held by both natives and non-natives. Native Area Land is land where individual land titles have been given to natives only. The State land is divided into Interior Area Land and Reserved Land. Native Customary Rights Land, where natives hold land under customary tenure, includes such land within areas which have been declared to be Mixed Zone Land or Native Area Land.

5 Dayak leaders are distributed in four major political parties in Sarawak: Sarawak National Party (SNAP), Parti Bumiputera Bersatu (PBB), Sarawak Chinese National Party (SUPP), and Parti Bansa Dayak Sarawak (PBDS). See Jawan (1993) on 'the Iban factor in Sarawak politics'.

6 See Ngidang's (1992:115-6) discussion of linkages and communication in relation to inter-agency coordination.

7 Abang Hj. A. Rauf (1992) explicitly advocates the government's transformation of VDSCs as a vehicle for rural development.

8 See research findings on the role of mass media in the diffusion of development information to the grassroots in Sarawak (Sharifah Mariam Ghazali, 1986), and also refer to Rauf's (1992) essay on the role of Village Development and Security Committees in Sarawak.

9 'Politics means deciding who gets what. It involves decisions about who is going to benefit, who isn't, and who is going to pay. Such decisions are never entirely rational.' (PASITAM, 1980)

10 Outpourings of public support for the policy of 'politics of development' have been published in local media (the *Borneo Post*, 22 July 1993; the *Sarawak Tribune*, 22 July 1993).

References

Colchester, M. (1991) 'A Future on the Land? Logging and the Status of Native Rights in Sarawak', *Malaysian Social Science Association*, pp 30/5/90: 36-45

Cramb, R. A. (1988) 'The Role of Smallholder Agriculture in the Development of Sarawak from 1963-88', paper presented at a seminar on the Development in Sarawak, Kuching, Sarawak

Chambers, R. (1983) *Rural Development: Putting the Last First*, London: Longman

Dandot, W.B. (1987) 'Large scale land development in Sarawak', *Journal AZAM*, 3: 3-21

Foo, A. and Henry L. (1991) 'Process of selection, surveying, acquisition and alienation of land for development in Sarawak', *Journal AZAM*, 8:34-54

Ghazali, S.M. (1986) 'The Role of Mass Media in the Diffusion of Development Information to the Grassroots in Sarawak', unpublished report, Kuching: Ministry of Social Development

Havelock, R.G. (1971) *Planning for Innovation Through Dissemination and Utilisation of Knowledge*, Ann Arbor, Michigan: The University of Michigan

Hong, E. (1987) *Natives of Sarawak, Survival in Borneo's Vanishing Forests*, Pulau Pinang: Social Institute

Jawan, J. (1993) *The Iban Factor in Sarawak*

Politics, Serdang, Selangor: University Pertanian Malaysia Press

Khan, A.H. (1975) 'The Comilla Experience in Bangladesh — My Lessons in Communication', paper presented on a conference on the Communication and Change in Developing Countries, Honolulu: East West-Center

King, V.T. (1987) 'Land settlement schemes and alleviation of rural poverty in Sarawak, East Malaysia: a critical commentary', *Southeast Asian Journal of Social Science*, 14: 71-99

King, V.T. (1988) 'Models and realities: Malaysian national planning and East Malaysian development problems', *Modern Asian Studies*, 22: 263-98

Leigh, M. (1988) 'Socio-political Dimension: Development in Sarawak', paper presented at a Seminar on the Development in Sarawak, Kuching, Sarawak

Mahmud, Hj. A. T. (1992) 'The politics of development: roles of and challenges for the elected representatives', *Journal AZAM*, 8:1-11

Melkote, S.R. (1987) 'Biases in development support communication: revealing the comprehensive gap', *Gazette*, 40: 39-55

Ngidang, D. (1992) 'Only in principles but not in practice: a dilemma of inter-agency coordination in extension', *Journal AZAM*, 8: 112-126

Ngidang, D., J. Uli, P. Songan, and S. Sanggin (1989) 'Common Features, Cultural Practices and Problems of the Pepper Cultivation in Serian District, Sarawak', unpublished report No. 3, Centre for Social Science and Management Studies, UPM Bintulu

PASITAM (1980) 'The politics of rural development: some lessons on the design process in development', Program of Advanced Studies in Institution Building and Technical Assistance Methodology, Indiana University, Bloomington, *Newsletter*, 1: 1-2

Rauf, Abang Hj. A. (1992) 'The roles of Village Development and Security Committees in Sarawak', *Journal AZAM* 8:71-111

Shamsul, A.B. (1989) 'Village: The Imposed Social Construct in Malaysia's Development Initiatives', working paper No. 115 in Southeast Asia Programme, Faculty of Sociology, University of Bielefeld, Germany

The author

Dimbab Ngidang is head of the Planning and Management Programme in the Faculty of Social Science at the Universiti Malaysia Sarawak.

This article first appeared in *Development in Practice* Volume 5, Number 4, in 1995.

What is development?

Hugo Slim

In hazarding a guess at what most of us in NGOs mean by development, I will try to sketch out the ideal as it has emerged in recent years and identify some of its essential ingredients. In so doing, I want to emphasise the following key principles:

- that genuine development is much more than a matter of economics and economic growth;
- that development is a universal goal for *all* societies and not just a 'Third World problem';
- that development depends on the just interaction between different groups and different nations, and that at the heart of the struggle for development is the struggle of relationships.

Having looked at the *ideal* of development and glimpsed a near-perfect world, I will then look briefly at the *reality* of the development agenda today, as it is dominated by the so-called 'Washington Consensus'. Finally, in the light of this reality I want to suggest that the right role for NGOs is one which continues to question current orthodoxy and, where appropriate, to seek alternatives to it.

What is development trying to do?

In 1974, a group of ten of the world's development experts (all men) met at Cocoyoc in Mexico to try to set a new agenda of 'alternative development', to move forward from what they considered to be the failure of development in the 1950s and 1960s. They produced the Cocoyoc Declaration, in which they made a basic distinction between priorities relating to the 'inner limits' and those relating to the 'outer limits' of development (Cocoyoc, 1974, pp.170-1).

The inner limits cover 'fundamental human needs' like food, shelter, health, and human rights. The outer limits relate to aspects of 'the planet's physical integrity' like the environment and population. This distinction is still a useful one and identifies the two great concerns of development: human development and protection of the planet, and their inevitable inter-dependence.

Some basic ingredients

In recent decades, development theorists and practitioners have come to recognise that a certain number of basic ingredients are required, if effective development is to take place within each of these two spheres. Listing some of these ingredients may help to give a picture of what development is and how it comes about.

Development is essentially about change: not just any change, but a definite improvement — a change for the better. At the same time, development is also about continuity. Because if change is to take root, it must have something in common with the community or society in question. It must make sense to people and be in line with their values and their capacity. Development must therefore be appropriate — culturally, socially, economically, technologically, and environmentally.

But appropriate does not means old-fashioned. Genuine development has an air of originality about it, but it is original not just by virtue of being novel. In the strict sense of the word, genuine development is original because it has its origins in that society or community, and is not simply an imported copy or imitation of somebody else's development. It is well known that 'imitative development' is often doomed to failure. At best it does not take root; at worst it imposes itself and distorts or destroys a society. Genuine development, therefore, is not about similitude and making everything the same. Instead, real development safeguards and thrives on difference, and produces diversity.

At the heart of any change for the better are the twin ingredients of equity and justice. Change will not be an improvement if it is built on injustice and does not benefit people equally. A quest for justice and equity usually meets resistance from some quarters, and this means that struggle, opposition, and conflict of some kind are also essential ingredients of development. This is because relationships are a major factor in determining develop-ment. Relationships between individuals, communities, the sexes, the social classes, and power groups combine with international relationships to dictate the equity of development throughout the world. Effective development will inevitably challenge some of these relationships in the process of changing them.

Participation is a critical aspect of equity. If development is really to belong to people, it must be shared by them. This means involving them. It is now a well-known maxim that true development can be achieved only *by people* and cannot be done *to people*. Representation and involvement in decision-making, action, and outcome are therefore regarded as essential. Many development theorists use the word 'democracy' to describe this process. And the idea of empowerment is increasingly used to describe the fulfilment of a participatory process, the consequence of which is the

achievement of other key development ingredients like choice, control, and access.

At the end of the day, development is judged as successful by whether or not it lasts. Sustainability, self-reliance, and independence are seen as vital ingredients in effective development: the eggs that bind the mixture of the cake. Sustainability is particularly important, because it guarantees a future for the improvements brought about by a community or society. Sustainability is therefore described as intergenerational equity, because the benefits of development will be equally available to future generations, and not all used up by the present generation. Effective development is about change for the better for future generations too, and not just at their expense.

If these are some of the ingredients of development, the oven in which they are all baked is time. Development takes time, and time is something of which Western culture in particular has very little. Most people agree that the pressure for quick results has been the cause of many of the world's most inappropriate development initiatives. It is a pressure which stems from a widespread naivety in the world's major development institutions over the last 50 years, a naivety founded on an over-confidence in technological and economic development, without sufficient regard for social and environmental realities.

Development is more than economics

Recognition of these various development ingredients has made it increasingly clear that there is more to human development than economic development. Real human development concerns more intangible factors that relate to the *quality* of change in people's lives, as well as to the *quantity* of change. This view that human development is more complex than economics alone is clearly expressed by John Clark in his 1991 book *Democratizing Development* (p. 36):

Development is not a commodity to be weighed or measured by GNP statistics. It is a process of change that enables people to take charge of their own destinies and realize their full potential. It requires building up in people the confidence, skills, assets and freedoms necessary to achieve this goal.

Economic growth is not a simple engine for human development. Development is not just about *having* more, but also about *being* more (Pratt and Boyden, 1985, CAFOD *et al.*, 1987). It is about developing the human person, human society, and the environment. One major trend in recent development theory and practice has been the merging of the human rights and environment agendas with the development agenda. This merger recognises that development must be valued in terms beyond simple economic analysis, and that poverty is as much about a loss of rights, freedom, culture, dignity, and environment as about low income. In his book *Empowerment: The Politics of Alternative Development* (1992), John Friedman outlines a new model of economic growth which takes human rights and the environment into account:

An appropriate economic growth path is pursued when market measures of production are supplemented with calculations of the probable social and environmental costs, or costs to third parties, that are likely to be incurred in any new investment.

The creation of UNDP's human develop-ment index (HDI) in 1990 was a further bold attempt to recognise that human develop-ment is more than economics, and is about the quality of human life as well as the quantity of economic growth. This point is well made in UNDP's 1993 *Human Development Report*:

There is no automatic link between income and human development. Several countries have done well in translating their income into the lives of their people: their human develop-ment rank is way ahead of their per capita income rank. Other societies have income ranks far above their human development rank, showing their enormous potential for improving the lives of their people.

The conclusion is that rich countries are not always the most developed, and poor countries are not always the least developed. Irresponsible economic growth — super-development — can act as a force for under-development in and against many societies. Civilisation (the old nineteenth-century word for development) is more than economic growth and is by no means a monopoly of the rich, but common to all societies.

A universal issue, not a 'Third World' issue

This de-linking of economic growth and human development brings the realisation that human-development strategies are required in response as much to over-development and super-development as to under-development. The extreme urbanisation, pollution, environmental degradation, unfair trading practices, and economic expansionism in European, North American, and South-East Asian societies are as much a form and cause of mis-development as the hunger, conflict, and poverty in some African, Asian, and Latin American societies.

Every society — rich or poor — has a development problem, and the old develop-ment geography of north/south, east/west, and of first, second, third, and fourth worlds, misses the point that fair and sustainable development is a global issue. As Friedman makes clear (1993, p. 131), human develop-ment is a challenge for world society:

Rich and poor countries constitute a single world system, and the overdevelopment of the first is closely linked to the misdevelopment of the second. Neither 'development' is sustain-able in the long run; and both fail to meet the equity test. A vision of alternative development is thus as pertinent for the countries central to the world economy as it is for those on the periphery.

Development is about relationships

Human relationships are one of the main determinants of human development. A great deal of the world's misdevelopment is the result of unfair or dysfunctional relationships at an international, national, or community level. At national and community levels, power relations, gender relations, and ethnic relations play a major part in shaping or distorting genuine development. At an international level, unjust economic relations ensnare poor countries into debt and commodity-pricing traps, while political imbalances prevent many countries from enjoying a full stake in global governance. In this context, much of what is offered as development aid is in fact a catalyst of misdevelopment, either because it is environmentally or socially inappropriate, or because its 'giving' represents the extension of a dysfunctional power relationship between nations. Because of this, Pope Paul VI wisely urged poor countries to 'choose with care between the evil and the good in what is offered by the rich' (CAFOD, 1967). The dysfunctional way in which the 'First World' projects so much of the shadow side of its psyche on to images of a 'weak and helpless Third World' also places huge cross-cultural obstacles in the way of healthy and just relationships between peoples.

Just human relationships are therefore one of the keys to development, and dialogue needs to be at the heart of the development relationship to encourage exchange, agreement, and partnership. For NGOs and other development organisations in particular, this question of forming just relations is crucial. As Charles Abrams has observed, effective co-operation between development professionals and the communities with which they work depends on recognising a place for the 'expert' from outside the community alongside the 'inpert' from inside it, and achieving the right balance between the two (Abrams, 1964).

Measuring development

The fact that development is an issue for every society, and that it is as much about human rights, the environment, and relationships as it is about economics, makes it an increasingly complex phenomenon to measure. The last few years have seen an enormous effort to move beyond traditional economic indicators (of production, income, consumption, debt, etc.) epitomised by the World Bank's world-development indicators, to a new broad range of indicators which capture the personal, social, cultural, and environmental dimensions of development.

Of this new generation of development indicators, the World Bank's programme of social indicators of development currently has 94 indicators and UNDP's Human Development Index (HDI) has 253 human-development indicators (UNDP, 1993). These range from infant mortality rates to air quality, through human rights, to TV ownership and population per passenger car. The HDI also claims to be gender-sensitive.

It is hard to gauge the accuracy and relevance of new development indicators like the HDI, which the British newspaper the *Daily Mail* described with typical tabloid precision as 'a happiness index'. However, they are at least evidence of the wider recognition that a purely economic model of development is not sufficient, and that in reality the quality and scope of development are more complex than the creation and distribution of wealth.

The reality of development today

Much of the above has described the ideal recipe for genuine development. In reality, however, the development menu today is dominated by one main dish, which is known as 'the Washington Consensus', served up from the policy kitchens of the White House, the World Bank, and the IMF in Washington, and garnished with the policies of the European Union.

With the end of the Cold War, the Western economic and political view has come to dominate the global scene. From living in a bi-polar world which set out two main models of political and economic development, we currently exist in an essentially uni-polar world, where the tenets of Western liberalism go unchallenged and dictate international policy. For the most part, the world now tends towards this view, which is therefore regarded as a consensus. Its motto is 'good governance', which has both economic and political aspects. Economic good governance refers to notions of free markets and a limited and enabling State. Political good governance is about human rights and the development of a vibrant society.

The Washington Consensus has much to commend it, and indeed co-opts a great deal of the language and ideas of previously progressive NGOs, especially relating to human rights, which somewhat takes the wind out of their sails as radical organisations. But in its ideals lie all the dangers of prescription and of a single model, because its whole platform hinges on the principle of conditionality. The Washington Consensus is a set menu, and it is now impossible for any aid-dependent country to order its development *à la carte*.

The set menu

The majority of Western aid is now conditional on the rigorous pursuance of good governance in its prescribed form. While there is little doubt that human rights are a given good and an ethical model to be applied across the world (although there is even some dispute about that), the same may not necessarily be the case for economic models and notions of the perfect State and society. For example, the enormous trust which the Washington Consensus places in civil society and a thriving NGO sector as a panacea for efficient service-provision may prove unfounded in the many different cultural and historical settings around the world. The informal voluntary sector is a peculiarly European (possibly even Anglo-Saxon) phenomenon which may not travel well.

There are, therefore, grave dangers in a single prevailing developmental model, particularly when — as is the case today — there is also a distinct lack of alternatives. The NGO sector, in particular, has always been the forum for opposition and alternative development strategies. Today it finds itself courted to an unprecedented degree by the establishment — often with echoes of its own words — and is in danger of being co-opted. But, as yet, it has no real alternatives to the Washington Consensus beyond a vague suspicion that the new blueprint of good governance cannot be any better than previous ones. This is not enough on which to make a stand, however, and in the meantime any debate about development seems to be suspended, with the argument temporarily won.

The case of Eastern Europe and the new States of the former Soviet Union adds a new financial urgency to the question. With Western aid budgets being reduced in real terms, it is alarming for development agencies concerned with Africa, Asia, and Latin America to see these dwindling budgets now being shared with the countries of Eastern Europe and the new independent States, especially when foreign policy is bound to dictate a priority for the former communist countries over and above other (most notably African) countries.

So what is development?

The first part of this article sketched out a relatively positive picture of what principles might be considered to contribute to genuine development. The ingredients it identified are complex and not easy to come by. Among them, the principles of diversity and originality were identified as essential, but the prospect for these two ingredients in particular appears even more distant in the light of the development *realpolitik* described above. The prevailing consensus prizes uniformity and only really allows for one road towards a single and over-prescribed model of development. It is perhaps ironic that a consensus which champions choice and the market in its economics tends not to encourage a market-place for developmental alternatives.

It seems fair to conclude that the main priority for the NGO community today is to continue to explore alternatives, and to question the current blueprint where it proves to be flawed, from the basis of experience and partnership. These alternatives should be used to influence and challenge current trends and, if not to change the model, at least to shape the best possible variations. Genuine universal development is indeed an ideal, a holy grail. But, as a general rule, it may be more creative to have several knights errant roaming the world in search of it in different ways and different places, instead of one white knight leading the whole band in one direction, in the belief that he knows where it is hidden.

Notes

This article is based on a Discussion Paper prepared for a Save the Children UK regional meeting in Thailand in December 1993. I am indebted to Douglas Lackey of SCF for setting me such a direct question as the subject of my session — a question that I had been happily dodging to date.

References

Abrams, C. (1964) *Man's Struggle for Shelter in an Urbanizing World*, Cambridge, Mass: MIT Press (quoted in N. Hamdi: *Housing Without Houses*, van Nostrand Reinhold, 1991).

CAFOD (1967) *This is Progress*, translation of the Encyclical Letter of Paul VI — *Populorum Progressio*, paragraph 41, London: CAFOD.

CAFOD et al. (1987) *Social Concern: A Simplified Version of the Encyclical Solicitudo Rei Socialis of John Paul II*, London: CAFOD.

Clark, J. (1991) *Democratizing Development: The Role of Voluntary Organizations*, London: Earthscan.

Cocoyoc Declaration (1974), quoted in Friedman (1992).

Friedman, J. (1992) *Empowerment: The Politics of Alternative Development*, Oxford: Blackwell.

Pratt, B. and J. Boyden (1985) *The Field Directors' Handbook*, Oxford: Oxfam (UK and Ireland).

UNDP (1993) *The Human Development Report*, Oxford: Oxford University Press.

The author

Hugo Slim is co-director of the Centre for Development and Emergency Planning (CENDEP), Oxford Brookes University. Previously he was Senior Research Officer at Save the Children Fund, and he has also worked in Morocco, Sudan, Ethiopia, Bangladesh, and the Occupied Territories.

This article first appeared in *Development in Practice* Volume 5, Number 2, in 1995.

Research into local culture:
implications for participatory development

Odhiambo Anacleti

Subjects or objects of development?

People in Africa are rarely asked what kind of development they want. They have always been the *objects* of various models, though these have rarely increased their supplies of food, or improved their state of health. Indeed, the poor in Africa have rarely been considered to be humans in their own right. They have always been the ones whom others would like to see changed, whether through Christianity, civilisation, research, or development projects. They are seldom thought to have a religion, a culture, or even a trading system of their own. They have to be initiated in all of this. They have to be helped, assessed, and given aid.

If the hope of a more equitable order is to be realised, attitudes towards the rural sector and rural people in developing countries need to undergo radical changes. It must be recognised that the rural sector (which is referred to here as 'local') has a dynamism of its own that does not have to be explained by comparison with, and in contrast to, external events and history. Rural people have their own concept of development, and have always been engaged in some kind of exchange of material goods and ideas with the outside. This already gives them a perception of the merits and demerits of such exchange. Such perceptions do not depend on how the world perceives and defines the concepts — but instead on how those concepts actually affect them.

Rural development must be seen as a process by which rural people avail themselves of an opportunity to upgrade their way of life, moving from mere strategies for survival to challenging the physical and social environment in which they find themselves. It is a process that enables them to become aware and to analyse the constraints to which they are subject. It is also a process that gives them access to the resources required for removing such constraints; and which acknowledges their right to plan and control their destiny in accordance with the resources available to them. To create equity, it must be appreciated that people, including rural people, do not wish others to define their needs for them. They can do it for themselves.

To recognise this implies a change in attitudes towards development; and, in turn, a need for information to identify the underlying causes behind the continued subservence of the rural sector to the towns and cities. Such information will provide the basis for creating alternative solutions to critical problems in the developing countries.

This is the only way open to us to reverse the extreme economic difficulties of the last three decades, which have had such devastating effects on the development potential of African rural people, and so undermined their political, economic, and cultural integrity — and even their identity. Collecting such information entails research into existing systems and institutions, and the possibilities for using these as the stepping stones towards development relevant for the people.

Why research into local culture?

We might question why anybody should recommend more research, given the amount of information available on practically every aspect of our lives! After all, increasing knowledge about the 'developing' countries and their poverty does not seem to have provided solutions to it. Is it because the information is irrelevant? Or is it because the solutions proposed are the wrong ones? Whatever the reason, I tend to the view that the researchers are asking the wrong questions.[1]

Community development is a process — and a rather slow one. It will be even slower if development agencies ignore Julius Nyerere's dictum that 'People are not developed, they develop themselves'.[2] But for people to develop themselves, they have to be convinced that the changes envisaged will not be a mere experiment with their lives, but will actually mean a change for the better.

People participate in what they know best. At present, and for the foreseeable future, at least 70 per cent of Africans will continue to be rural and semi-literate. Their knowledge will continue to be parochial, but specific to the realities of their daily lives. Most of this knowledge will continue to be transmitted through tradition from one generation to another. The tradition will continue to be guided mainly by cultural principles and values. Hence the need to study local culture as the starting point for dialogue about people's development and their participation in bringing it about.

Practically all rural communities still cherish their culture, as manifested by their traditional knowledge, skills, values, customs, language, art forms, organisation and management systems, and institutions: these are what have enabled them to survive as communities in a physical and social environment that is sometimes very hostile. It seems obvious that research should be focused on developing this culture. The tendency, however, has been towards finding alternatives to what people already have, rather than on identifying where the inadequacies lie and improving on them. It is no wonder that communities often respond negatively when they are expected to implement the research findings of development theorists: it often seems to them that the proposed solutions would alienate them from the very culture which they value.

It is ironic, but true, that colonial governments (for example in the case of Tanzania mainland, and other former African colonies) were more conscious of this than independent governments. Colonial officials were very aware of the importance of knowing the culture of the people, presumably reasoning that if they did not control people's cultural behaviour, they would never rule them. Speculation aside, they did quite a lot of work in trying to understand the native systems, and even applying them in day-to-day administration.

One such example is Hans Cory's study[3] of the Kuria of Tanzania's Tarime district, which was used in establishing the system of chieftaincy which transcended the traditional clans, and is still in use today. As one Tanzanian Regional Commissioner told me: 'The colonial DC travelled more miles per year in his district than the current Tanzanian DCs do in their Land Rovers.'[4] This gave the colonial authorities a close insight into the culture of local communities, which they would then apply in organising their rule over the people. Could the current administrators not imitate this?

The success of any effort to do so would depend on two factors. First, understanding people's culture requires some degree of humility on the part of the researchers, since they are required to confess ignorance about the subject of their research. Many would-be researchers fear exposing their ignorance of the specific systems. It is easier, after all, to assume that all rural areas are similar, and whatever is true for rural Malawi will apply to rural Kenya.

The second factor militating against research into local culture is the assumption by indigenous researchers that because they are natives, they already understand the culture. These people forget that their socialisation process in their own communities was not completed, because of the short spans of time they spent there once they began attending school. Besides, being indigenous usually limits the kinds of question they may ask, as they will be supposed by the communities to know the answers already. Being indigenous can be more of a hindrance than a help to cultural research; and the researcher needs to be conscious of this fact.

I know you do not know what I know, but why do you not want to know that I too know what you do not know? You may have quite a lot of book knowledge, but I still believe (olul ok puonj dhok mit chiemo) that the anus does not teach the mouth the sweetness of food.[5]

Such was the exasperation of Mzee Joel Kithene Mhinga of Buganjo village in north Tanzania, expressed after a long discussion in which I tried to prove to him that he had got his historical facts wrong about the genesis of the Baganjo clan. It reminded me of another argument in a workshop held in Dodoma to train traditional birth attendants. The village women were protesting at being called 'traditional' and 'attendants'. They wondered why the formally trained midwives wanted to monopolise the word 'midwife', when they were sure they had delivered more live children than any nurse present. As a compromise, they agreed to be called 'traditional midwives', provided that the hospital midwives agreed to be called 'pen midwives'.[6]

It is not often that rural people will express themselves so candidly. But the truth remains that the traditional knowledge which has enabled the communities to survive has often been ignored in preference to book learning. Researchers and development agents have presumed to know the inner thinking and behaviour of illiterate rural people, even when they do not know enough. And because they fail to understand what rural people know, they tend to compensate for this with something new, rather than proving the inadequacy of the existing knowledge, systems, and institutions. Local knowledge has been undervalued for too long — to the detriment of the development of the rural people and their countries.

Although history has proved that alien ideas imposed on people always end in failure, there is still great faith in the imposition of development models, supposedly successful elsewhere, on other people without their consent. This happens despite people's resistance to such imposition. We should reflect on the example of Minigo village in Tarime district, Tanzania, where in 1986 the men refused manually powered grinding mills because (according to the Chief) 'it would make their wives lazy'. In fact, they were trying to convey their feeling that the time of manual grinding mills had passed. They were hoping that if they refused them, then the donors would give them a diesel-powered grinding mill which would not only help the women but would also bring revenue to the village.

For people to participate in decisions that affect their lives, they must start from where they are and with what they know. What most people know is their own culture and values. Hence in order to liberate people from imposed, impractical, and often unproved systems and institutions, they need to be involved in integrating those systems into their culture, in the search for alternatives within their cultural milieu.

The relevance of participatory development

'Participatory development' implies development which involves all the people, especially those whose basic needs and aspirations are affected by the decisions concerning the availability of resources and entitlement to such needs. Participatory development, therefore, includes equitable sharing of the control, division, and use of the resources and of the ultimate benefits of development in a community. It also involves taking responsibility and being accountable to the community at all levels. This will be just wishful thinking if the decision-making structures remain alien, bureaucratic, and elitist. Rather, they must be made more comprehensible and acceptable to the people. The best way of doing this is to look at existing cultural systems and integrate the decision-making structures into them.

In 1973, the Tanzanian government decided to settle its population in villages. The aim was to make Tanzanians live like a traditional African family which 'lived together and worked together', to achieve the objective of building 'a society in which all members have equal rights and equal opportunities; in which all can live at peace with their neighbours without suffering or imposing injustice, being exploited or exploiting; and in which all have a gradually increasing basic level of material welfare before any individual lives in luxury.'[7] If the plan had been implemented properly, it would have come very close to achieving what is implied by participatory development. What actually happened was that cultural implications were not taken into consideration. For instance, there was no local research to find out what forms of working together were still in existence, and how they fitted into a pattern in which individuals were producing their own individual cash crops. The type of 'Ujamaa' living envisaged would have been possible only under the communal system of land ownership which was no longer extant in Tanzania. An examination of the way in which people had adopted and organised new patterns of land ownership would have helped to increase the social and economic acceptability of the whole operation. As this was not done, it was no wonder that 'villagisation' was regarded as coercive behaviour on the part of the government, in its attempt to show that it ruled over (rather than belonged to) the people.

This is a good example of a situation in which concern for and awareness of people's culture and customs would have gone a long way to achieving participatory change. No wonder that 20 years ater people are going back to their old homesteads and re-creating their own structures, which could have informed the authorities of 20 years ago. What a waste!

Involving people in discussing their own development, and arriving at decisions, leads to an understanding of why engagement in the whole process of problem-solving is necessary to bring about lasting and worthwhile change. The current process is that researchers and development agents claim to be representatives of the people, on the arrogant assumption that their particular techniques are the exclusive domain of trained academics and elites. This ignores the fact that they depend on local people to achieve their goals.

People, in the last analysis, are the repository of local knowledge. In order to help them to develop, they must be enabled to tap that knowledge. The best way to do this is to help them extrapolate from what they know best, their culture. In doing so, they will able to relate their deeply felt aspirations to the surrounding social reality. This connection is so rarely made by development agents that people are usually seen as just another resource for development, rather the subjects of their own development.

Notes

1 An idea explained very well by Michael Edwards, Oxfam's former Representative in Zambia, in his paper 'The Irrelevance of Development Studies' (mimeo 1979).
2 J. K. Nyerere: *Freedom and Socialism* (Oxford: Oxford University Press, 1978).
3 This study, written in 1948, is stored in the Tanzania National Archives.
4 P. Syovelwa, visiting Hadzabe village, 1979.
5 Personal communication, , 1979.
6 Training workshop for Traditional Birth Attendants, Mvumi Hospital, 1986.
7 Nyerere, op. cit.

The author

Odhiambo Anacleti works for Oxfam (UK and Ireland) as Communications Officer (Africa); previously he was the Area Coordinator for Africa South, and the Country Representative in Tanzania. Before that, he was Director of Research and Planning at the Tanzanian Ministry of National Culture and Youth, and lectured at the University of Dar es Salaam Institute of Development Studies.

This article first appeared in *Development in Practice*, Volume 3, Number 1, in 1993.

An education programme for peasant women in Honduras

Rocío Tábora

Now I feel I have the inner strength, the belief that I am capable, and that what I think will be taken seriously. When I think now, I do so in the confidence that I am a person in my own right. (Honduran peasant woman)

Introduction

Over the last ten years, the social and economic situation in Honduras has worsened in every respect. Many of the political models so faithfully adopted in the past have become obsolete in today's context. At the same time, the neo-liberal truths and certainties currently fashionable are every day belied by their own failure to resolve basic social problems — and by the increased wretchedness, delinquency, and suffering which make us feel so confused and powerless.

Against this background, and given the authoritarianism of our cultural heritage, we urgently need to develop a culture of democracy, in which differences are respected and where solidarity is encouraged. As Ibanez, the Peruvian educationalist, writes:

What we are talking about is a new way of living; new social relations, ways of working, thinking, feeling, celebrating ... social change requires us to change our own daily lives ... we can't divorce one plane from another.[1]

The various centres and NGOs in Central America which work with the 'popular sectors'

are, along with ordinary people themselves, having to rethink their own aspirations. We are having to redefine our roles as support institutions, and look again at how we engage with grassroots communities. We have to learn how to value and draw on the significant experience in teaching and learning which people have already developed, for themselves, with or without our help. A particularly encouraging example of such educational and organisational work is being undertaken by a women's education programme (PAEM) in north-west Honduras.

What is PAEM?

PAEM is a programme which has developed among Christian women in the rural parishes of Santa Barbara, Colon, Comayagua, Intibuca, and Lempira Departments. Its overall aims are:

- To bring together women who are already involved in activities run by the Roman Catholic church, as well as any other disadvantaged women from nearby peasant communities.
- To create an alternative approach to educational and organisational work with women which is responsive to their specific problems, needs, and concerns.
- To contribute to establishing a distinctive sense of what it means to be a woman in Central and Latin America.
- To engage in discussions on the subjects of

gender, social class, and ethnicity, as well as the specific role of women in bringing about social change, both with the Church authorities and with the leadership of the popular movement.

- To create a space for women, based on their own identity and equality as human beings, as the basis for them to contribute fully and autonomously to creating a society marked by justice, humanity, and solidarity.

PAEM's methodological contribution

In COMUNICA (the NGO Centre for Communication and Training for Development) we aim to develop a clear methodology for strengthening communication work within the social organisations with whom we work. We have been enriched by our working contact with PAEM in every way, both personally and professionally. Over the last three years, COMUNICA has been able to draw on the strength of the women in PAEM; and to learn something about how academic and practical ways of understanding the world can complement each other. We have been able to live at first hand, through PAEM, some of the theoretical debates that are shaping new ideas about popular education in Latin America: namely, the crucial importance of the individual or person: seeing his or her subjectivity and feelings as part of our culture, and what that means.

In the case of the peasant women in PAEM, we have seen repeatedly how their feelings impinge on all the educational work. In fact, the teaching materials themselves revolve around three basic questions: *How do we live? How do we think? What do we feel?*

Women, communication, and culture

With PAEM, we have come to see how traditional forms of expression — dance, poetry, customs, story-telling — can themselves be woven into an authentic form of popular communication. It is far more impor- tant to begin by looking at how people *actually* communicate, than to make elaborate assumptions from the outside about how they *ought* to communicate.

Communication and everyday life are, in reality, on a continuum. But we so often distort this when we come in from the outside and insist on our way of doing things. For example, we have a quite different notion of time and space, or of what constitutes appropriate behaviour. We have tight schedules: we don't allow for long silences, for changing the baby's nappy, or trying to do three things at once. We take advantage of being articulate and tend to dismiss the immediacy of life, or of just being together: we dichotomise training and recreation.

At the same time, the cultural repression of women, our marginalisation in society and throughout history, have had (and continue to have) many consequences. One of these is that women have been inhibited and so prevented from developing the ability to communicate as effectively as they would like. Women have difficulty in expressing themselves; in experiencing and communicating, whether in words, feelings or physical expression. Women have been denied the right to be creative, thus limiting the role they could be playing in putting forward their own alternatives in the process of social change.

To reverse this process of marginalisation, we women have to look deep inside ourselves in order to unravel the threads which tie us down and keep us subordinate. We have to recognise the subjectivity and feelings which criss-cross the decisions and beliefs which predominate in our minds at a rational level. In other words, it is crucial that we get to know ourselves as women.

For peasant women, already facing so much insecurity and uncertainty, economically dependent on men and with relatively few employment opportunities, this process of self-assertion is immensely harder. Yet for six years, PAEM has been working from the premise that, for women, self-esteem has to be the inspiration or starting-point for any genuine educational work.

These women have gradually reclaimed the right to laugh, to talk, to have fun, to share, to have self-esteem and dignity — in short, to live.

The emphasis on human, democratic values marks PAEM out as a space where women can lose the fear of making a mistake or being wrong. Here, they can learn to take on a more assertive role in their communities and to participate in, and run, their own social organisation; and they can recognise the resistance and barriers which they all experience for what they are.

PAEM's starting point for action is the self-denigration and self-marginalisation which women have to overcome in order to speak, put forward ideas, and genuinely participate in the search for a different future. In Latin American societies, which are so profoundly patriarchal, authoritarian, and non-participative, our feelings are constantly denied:

We live in a culture which devalues emotions in direct proportion to the over-valuing of reason, in our wish to distinguish ourselves from other animals, as rational beings.[2]

Challenges and perspectives

Even in the field of popular education, emotions are, more often than not, seen as getting in the way of understanding, or constraining our rational thought-processes. Feelings are generally identified as falling within the feminine realm. As Burin argues,

Women, through the experience of mother-hood, develop the capacity to care for others, using our communication skills as a means to resolve disagreements. These are in fact qualities which every human being needs; however, within our culture, they are not seen as something which has to be learned the hard way, but rather as something 'naturally' feminine. Since these qualities are not socially valued, they are not fully included in our understanding of what constitutes emotional maturity and mental health.[3]

In both the content and the methodology of PAEM's work, unexpressed emotions are seen as being the key to women's being able to revalue themselves. We would do well to adopt this approach in other educational work, given that our feelings do in fact underlie our values, our expressions of solidarity with others, and our sense of human dignity. We need to see ourselves as thinking *and* feeling beings. Giving recognition to our emotions in the educational work we do is the way to make it both more human and, paradoxically, more objective. Given the exaggerated form of masculinity, *machismo*, which dominates us, to accord a proper place to so-called femininity is actually a way for us all to make our everyday social relations more democratic.

Today, NGOs which are involved in education are having to be much clearer about their theoretical assumptions, and about the specific needs of the children, women, and men with whom they aim to work. In view of the crisis affecting the popular education 'movement', we need more than ever before to analyse, order, and interpret our practical experience. Patience in this task is crucial. What we have to remember above all is that people already have their own experience, knowledge and understanding, gained from their daily lives or involvement in social organisations. We need to look afresh at the people we claim to help, and see how we can build on their existing experience in developing, validating, and strengthening our methodologies.

As we in COMUNICA have worked alongside PAEM, we have seen how democracy is constructed at the micro-level. Discovering their own voice is what allows women to participate in an authentic way. The echoes are to be heard in the everyday sphere: husbands and partners learning to see their wives as thinking human beings, with their own rights, and so taking on some of the domestic chores; priests and lay-workers allowing themselves to be interrupted by women; women who will fight for and defend their space, their autonomy, and their identity. All these are encouraging signs in a world of poverty and despair.

Such minute expressions of change are the basis for grassroots alternatives in which men and women participate fully. And, in the overall process of democratisation in Central America, people who have always been relegated to an inferior position must now begin to demand the power they have historically been denied. Women, especially peasant women, need to start by insisting on their own 'space' in every quarter: the family, the community, the cooperative, the trade union or social organisation, and so on. Only if women, along with all the other disadvantaged groups, begin to do this will we really be able to build a viable alternative to the authoritarian social structures which have successfully dehumanised us for so long.

Oral tradition and gender issues

In our own work with women, we at COMUNICA has made great use of videos in building on our oral tradition as a means of raising gender-related issues. These are my particular areas of expertise, but it is also well known that ours is a pre-eminently oral tradition. In the rural areas and poorer town districts, as soon as the sun goes down, the streets, patios, and pavements are meeting places: places to laugh, and share anxieties, anecdotes, and jokes. Our oral tradition is rich in magical stories, fantasies, and legends. But we should not ignore the fact that these creations are also a means by which ideas, beliefs, and stereotypes are transmitted. As such, they tend to reflect prevailing attitudes to those disadvantaged by our society: ethnic minorities, disabled people, women.

In general, popular education programmes have been incapable of drawing on the richness of our narrative traditions, their evocative and inspiring strength. In just the same way, formal education has disregarded literature as a source of knowledge. Once again, life and education are dichotomised. Imagination, fantasy, and feeling are seen as pointless and a waste of time. Hence the chance for people to develop

their creative potential, their appreciation and enjoyment of language and imagery through education, is reduced.

The use of traditional forms of story-telling helps us to unravel, examine, and re-order the threads which bind our consciousness and which condition the way in which we see, feel and respond to the world. It can help us to consider our prejudices and analyse the myths and beliefs which can divide or unite us: we can recognise our own richness and so strengthen our identities.

If we look at the contents of many narratives within the peasants' own story-telling tradition, we can easily identify those elements which stereotype women and reinforce their self-deprecation. These images become the daily reality for women who are oppressed and subordinated. None the less, we can develop practical insights from reflecting on these stories along with peasant women. For example, some of the exercises we have used in our work with PAEM have been based on the following approach:

- A woman tells a story.
- The group recreates the story, perhaps adding their own version of it.
- We discuss what we think and feel about the narrative, and what identification with the characters has taken place.
- We talk about the symbols and beliefs represented in the story, including their theological significance. (This is especially relevant, given the strong Christian influence in oral peasant tradition.)
- We analyse the social implications of what took place in the story: what kind of human relations are depicted, and whose interests do they serve?
- We draw conclusions and consider what practical application they might have in our lives and work.

In COMUNICA, we are now increasingly drawing in this way on the oral tradition in our own thinking on popular education and communication work. For myself, my own subjective experience of working with

Honduran peasant women has enabled me to recreate my own vision of Utopia, and helped me more fully to engage with a country which (in the words of the Peruvian writer Arguedas and the Cuban poet-singer Rodriguez) 'keeps us hovering between terror and hope ... between fear and tenderness'.

Notes

1 Alfonso Ibanez, 'Alcances politicos y culturales de la educación popular', *Contexto y Educao*, Number 23, July-Sept. 1991, p.10.
2 Humberto Maturana R., *Emociones y lenguaje en educación y politica: Educación y comunicación*, (2nd edition), Colección Hachette-Comunicación, Chile, 1990, p.14.
3 Mabel Burin, *Estudios sobre la subjetividad feminina: Mujeres y salud mental*, Grupo Editor Latinoamericano, Colección Controversia, Buenos Aires, 1987, pp. 397-8.

The author

Rocío Tábora is a psychologist and currently the Director of COMUNICA (Centro de Comunicación y Capacitación para el Desarrollo), Honduras. She is the author of *Fotografía y educación de adultos: Algunas reflexiones sobre la comunicación visual*, COMUNICA-CEAAL, 1991; and *Democratizando la vida: La propuesta metodologica de las mujeres del PAEM*, COMUNICA-PAEM, 1992.

This article was translated from Spanish by Deborah Eade, and first appeared in *Development in Practice*, Volume 3, Number 1 in 1993.

Challenging gender stereotypes in training:
Mozambican refugees in Malawi

Lewis B Dzimbiri

Background

The phenomenon of Mozambican refugees in Malawi dates back to the time of Portuguese colonial rule. However, it is the spectacular magnitude of today's influx which has attracted national and international attention. By the close of 1992, Malawi — whose national population is about nine million — was hosting over one million Mozambican refugees in 12 of the 24 districts.

This paper grew out of an ethnographic study conducted by the Universities of Oxford and Malawi, with the overall objective of examining the motives for and the impact of the provision of humanitarian assistance on the refugees and host-country populations (Zetter 1991). The writer, whose focus was the organisation and management of the refugee regime, held extensive discussions with representatives of the entire range of government and NGO agencies involved, as well as with refugees, in two camps — Chifunga in Mwanza and Tengani in Nsanje — and two self-settled areas of Ntcheu and Dedza, all focused on skills-development among refugees, to promote sustainable socio-economic development.

The central argument of this paper is that by applying traditional ideas about men's and women's roles to the recruitment of trainees for income-generating activities, women's development potential remains largely untapped. Alternative approaches to working with women have to be *actively* sought, to ensure that the process of development is fruitful as well as gender-fair.

Women in development and relief programmes

The socio-economic role of women throughout rural Africa and elsewhere is crucial. It is estimated that women are responsible for about 70 per cent of staple food production, as well as for household management, child-care, gathering wood, drawing water, and pounding grain, among other household tasks.

Despite this, women are conspicuously neglected in development and relief initiatives, with most benefits tending to accrue to men. Women are marginalised in education, skills-training, and decision-making. According to the famous African leader, Dr Aggrey, when you educate a man, you have educated an individual; but when you educate a woman, you have educated a family (Castle 1965). For development to be realistic as well as significant, women should be central to any development strategy.

Worldwide, women and children constitute approximately 80 per cent of the global refugee population (Meier-Braun 1992). For example, at Muloza Camp in Mulanje District in Malawi, Machika (1992) found that of the total population of 32,430, 52 per cent were children and 26 per cent women, while 22 per cent (6,907) were men. Of the women, evidence shows that most are single: widows, divorcées, or deserted wives (Kalyati 1990), with children.

Paradoxically, in spite of their numerical majority among the adult population, women refugees are marginalised. The failure to recognise either their pivotal position in the household economy or their specific needs has led not only to putting refugee women at a disadvantage, but has meant also that whole programmes have gone awry. Thus, policy makers and field workers alike unknowingly or deliberately contribute further to the weakening of women's position (Harrell-Bond 1986).

Refugee women and the camp context

Before seeking refuge in Malawi, about 90 per cent of Mozambican refugees were involved in some kind of agricultural activity, in which women participated in cultivation, planting, weeding, and harvesting (Kotch 1990, Machika 1992). Unfortunately, the expanded agricultural programmes are not possible in the camp context. So in order to strengthen the spirit of self-reliance among refugee populations, emphasis is put on non-agricultural income-generating activities, such as tailoring, carpentry, tin-smithing, bread-making, mat-making, shoe repairs, sewing, and knitting. This is not to suggest that there are no agriculture-related activities. Far from it. There is, for instance, some vegetable growing and small-animal husbandry. However, the strategy of focusing on non-agricultural activities raises many questions. To what extent are refugee populations achieving self-reliance? How many people overall are involved as beneficiaries? Further, given that such activities may not absorb everyone, because of the 'narrow gate' through which beneficiaries are recruited (Dzimbiri 1992), what is the ratio between men and women in various projects? If the role of women is central to the livelihood of a household, how much is done to enhance the earning capacities of refugee women? What is the role

of gender in the allocation of projects and the recruitment of beneficiaries?

Refugee women and projects: an overview

This section presents a selected typology of women's involvement in various income-generating projects, using data supplied by project coordinators and field supervisors. Two NGOs illustrate the case of Chifunga Camp in Mwanza, and three illustrate the case of Tengani Camp in Nsanje.

Chifunga Camp

1 Save the Children Fund (Malawi): vegetable growing

Beneficiaries	Men	Women
300	240	60

2 Christian Council of Malawi: poultry and carpentry

Project	Beneficiaries	Men	Women
Poultry	12	9	3
Carpentry	14	14	0
Totals:	26	23	3

Tengani Camp

1 Evangelical Alliance for Relief and Development (EVARD): tin-smithing and home economics

Project	Beneficiaries	Men	Women
Tin-smithing	240	240	0
Home economics	30	0	30
Totals:	270	240	30

2 Save the Children Fund (Malawi): vegetable growing

Beneficiaries	Men	Women
912	703	209

3 Christian Council of Malawi: various

Project Beneficiaries		Men	Women
Poultry	15	10	5
Mat-making	20	20	0
Tailoring	7	7	0
Radio repairs	5	5	0
Rabbit-rearing	6	6	0
Shoe repairs	1	1	0
Totals:	54	49	5

Thus, of a total of 1,562 beneficiaries in the various income-generating activities in the two camps, only 307 women refugees participated, less than 20 per cent of the total adult population. Furthermore, while no women took part in tin-smithing, carpentry, mat-making, tailoring, and radio or shoe repairs, there were no men participating in 'home economics' activities. Are NGOs just reinforcing the 'traditional' division of labour among men and women?

In the writer's experience, these two camps are by no means unique. If recruitment of beneficiaries is based on preconceived traditional (or archaic) notions of a gender-stereotyped distinction between men and women, many refugee women will fall into a state of helplessness and enforced idleness, since the camp environment severely restricts farming activities. Among married women, one can speculate that their husbands may be incorporated in other projects. But the situation bears hard on the majority of single or unaccompanied women, not all of whom are beneficiaries even of the so-called 'women in development' projects such as knitting or sewing.

Worse still, even if women are included in them, these activities are not in great demand, given the real-life situation of the refugee population. Do they really need table mats, or cloths? If not, then there is no demand for them — hence they cease to be income-generating! For instance, while UNHCR places large orders for school uniforms made by tailoring groups, school desks and chairs made by carpenters, and pails made by tin-

smiths, it does not commission table mats or cloth made by refugee women. If the objective of these activities were just occupational, rather than to make money for survival beyond 'hand-outs', then this might cause less concern. But should we condemn refugee women to activities which cannot strengthen their self-reliance?

The picture of the narrower gate for women on the path towards self-reliance becomes increasingly clear when one observes the statistics of women beneficiaries in activities that are truly income-generating.

It is against this scenario that the writer believes that emphasis should be shifted *deliberately* across traditional lines to give women increased participation in meaningful economic activities. We must match practice with theory in promoting equal opportunities for men and women.

The Norwegian Refugee Council (NRC)

The overall objective of NRC is to enhance self-reliance through skills development among Mozambican refugees and Malawians affected by the influx of Mozambican refugees. In Ntcheu, NRC has two project sites, Biriwiri and Kambironjo, where it has taken a decision to involve women in traditionally male-dominated skill areas — as illustrated below:

Biriwiri Project Site

Project Beneficiaries		Men	Women
Tin-smithing	22	5	17
Tailoring	25	10	13
Bricklaying	8	5	3
Carpentry	10	5	5
Bee-keeping	32	0	32
Totals:	97	25	72

Kambironjo Project Site

Project	Beneficiaries	Men	Women
Tailoring	22	8	14
Carpentry	16	10	0
Fish-farming	14	4	10
Bee-keeping	104	34	70
Tin-smithing	20	12	8
Mushroom-growing	8	0	8
Totals:	184	68	116

Here, women represent over 74 per cent and 63 per cent of the total project beneficiaries respectively. It is fascinating to learn how projects *can* be designed to increase the involvement of women in key or lucrative activities, in spite of deep-rooted cultural norms and expectations. How did the NRC make this important breakthrough?

Originally, women were reluctant to join male-dominated trades such as carpentry, tin-smithing, and brick-laying. However, a systematic awareness-raising process helped to shift women's values and beliefs. Teaching aids included posters or newspaper cuttings showing women in trades such as engineering, carpentry, welding, architecture, tin-smithing, and so on. This created a great stir among Mozambican refugee women and their Malawian counterparts. Since then, these projects have never been starved of new recruits. According to Norman Tembo, the field supervisor at Biriwiri, 'Our problem now is how to accommodate the many women refugees on the waiting list, which is quite substantial all the time.' It is also pleasing to note that UNHCR creates markets for these beneficiaries by placing large orders for water buckets, school uniforms, and desks.

Is this approach not worth emulating and improving? It is not too late. After all, as Robert Chambers (in Harrell-Bond 1986) remarks, the intractable problem of millions of refugees, displaced persons, and victims of famine in rural Africa and elsewhere will not go away.

Conclusion

There is an urgent need to shift the traditional gender-biased approaches in allocating projects among beneficiaries among long-stay refugees. Since the camp environment restricts agricultural activity, skills-development among refugee women should focus on real income-generating activities, even if these are considered the traditional domain of men. The example of the Norwegian Refugee Council in Malawi is a good starting point.

References

Castle, E.B., 1965, *Principles of Education for Teachers in Africa*, London: Oxford University Press.

Dzimbiri L.B., 1992, 'Managing Refugees in Malawi — An Overview', unpublished Research Report, Zomba: Chancellor College.

Harrell-Bond, B.E., 1986, *Imposing Aid: Emergency Assistance to Refugees*, Oxford: Oxford University Press.

Kotch A.B., 1990, 'Refugee Women in Malawi: Their Role in Household Food Security', EGM/RDWC/1990/BP2 Vienna June 28.

Machika, M.R.E., 1992, 'Income Generation Activities among Camp Refugees — the Case of Muloza Camp', Blantyre: conference paper.

Meier-Braun K.H., 1992, 'The new mass migration', *Scala Magazine*, September/October 1992.

Zetter, R., 1991, 'Governments, NGOs and Humanitarian Assistance for Refugees in Southern Africa: Handbook for Researchers', Oxford University.

The author

Lewis B. Dzimbiri is a Lecturer in Public Administration at the University of Malawi. This article first appeared in *Development in Practice*, Volume 5, Number 2, in 1995.

Defining local needs:
a community-based diagnostic survey in Ethiopia

Yezichalem Kassa and Feleke Tadele

Introduction

Oxfam in Ethiopia has long been concerned that community-based development programmes should reflect local felt needs and priorities. Particularly where there has been a long history of engagement in a given area, a diagnostic survey has proved to be a valuable and flexible self-monitoring tool to re-assess development objectives with community groups.

A diagnostic survey uses Rapid Rural Appraisal techniques in a series of dialogues and interactions. The intention of the survey described here was to determine whether the development programmes of Dubbo Catholic Mission (mother and child health services and water supply) were appropriate development activities for communities which had not previously been involved.

Background

The Franciscan Missionaries of Our Lady at the Catholic Church Mission, Dubbo have been running a Mother and Child Health (MCH) outreach programme with the rural com-munities in Bolosso Suri *wereda* (district) in Wollayita Region for 23 years. Oxfam has provided funding and institutional support for various programme components since 1974. Alongside this, a rural water-supply programme was established in 1984, aimed at protecting springs to improve the quality and quantity of domestic water supply. Oxfam is still funding both programmes.

The current phase of the MCH programme covers 18 peasant associations (PAs) from five health posts, with a total eligible population of 5,620 children under five years of age. The programme works closely with the regional and district offices of the Ministry of Health. Health assistants from the District Health Centre at Areka accompany Dubbo MCH staff to outreach sites and also vaccinate all children under one year of age. Serious cases and high-risk pregnant women are referred by programme staff to Areka Health Centre.

During 1993, administrative changes within the Bolosso Suri *wereda* resulted in the Areka Health Centre taking on responsibilities for Dangara Salata and Dangara Madelcho PAs. The two communities were incorporated into the Dubbo MCH programme from January 1994, following a diagnostic survey. This was undertaken by Dubbo Mission staff as a training exercise, and was facilitated by Oxfam.

Survey findings

Dangara Salata and Dangara Madelcho PAs are situated some 15km north-west of Areka, the principal town of Bolosso Suri *wereda*. Apparently they were inhabited 150 years ago by a chief named Dangara. When the PAs were formed with their present boundaries, they were named after the chief's two older sons: Salata and Madelcho.

The current population of Dangara Salata and Dangara Madelcho PAs is estimated to be 9,537 and 8,600 people respectively, with an average household size of seven. Most inhabitants are of Wollaita ethnic origin and are Christians who have affiliations with Ethiopian Orthodox, Catholic, and Protestant Churches.

Considerable change has occurred in the socio-economic patterns of the people living in the PA areas. There is now dense human settlement, severe shortages of cultivable land, and few opportunities for off-farm activities. This was illustrated by the local people through a line history exercise.

Transect walk and work patterns

Alolla river, which is the main water-source for both livestock and domestic purposes, forms the western boundary of the two PAs. Maps of the physical environment were drawn with groups of men and women. Available water sources, gullies, crop lands, trees, roads, offices, and residences of Traditional Birth Attendants and circumcisers were indicated on the maps.

An analysis of the agricultural production systems practised by farmers and the work patterns and labour requirements of cultivation was also compiled with groups of men and women. Four seasons were clearly identifiable, according to the work pattern of the predominantly farming households.

Most families tend to build their grass-thatched houses on their private farm land. Their landholdings do not usually exceed half a hectare, which is apportioned to up to 18 types of crops. For example, one farmer grows enset (false banana), taro, sweet potato, cabbage, sugar cane, banana, orange, avocado, hops, coffee, haricot bean, maize, teff, sorghum, barley, and various herbs.

Livestock herds of limited size graze on common land. Small stock and calves were tethered around some homesteads.

Constraints on agricultural production

Groups of men and women identified their main problems as follows:

High population pressure

Community groups pointed out that the number of families depending on available land resources is greater than the carrying capacity of the land. Most young men have limited opportunities for farm employment. Out-migration, which was possible in the past, is now hampered both by limited employment prospects in urban areas, and by lack of confidence to move from one region to another because of the government's ethnically-based regionalisation policy.

High rainfall variability

The PAs have experienced uncertain rainfall patterns in the last two years, when the seasons have started and finished earlier. The community groups stated that this has caused a change of crops planted, and in their view a waste of agricultural inputs. Farmers have adjusted to the changes by planting drought-tolerant crops of enset, sweet potato, banana and coffee, by inter-cropping, and by relying on more early-maturing crops which require fertilisers.

Limited land holdings

The average land-holding in the PAs does not exceed half a hectare per household. When a male family member marries, family land-holdings are re-apportioned. Out-migration to seek seasonal farm-labouring work is used to supplement production on the small land-holdings.

Crop pests and diseases

Sweet-potato butterfly is a scourge of one of the staple crops in the two PAs. Pesticides have to be purchased to control the larvae.

Loss of soil fertility

The farmers can neither expand their land-holdings nor exploit them. There is a general understanding that better production could be achieved if land could be left fallow. Poor extension services, insecurity of land tenure and ownership, and the tripling in the purchase price of fertiliser following the devaluation of the Ethiopian Birr were all cited as constraints on land fertility.

Lack of oxen

A draught animal is the biggest asset for a household, as confirmed in the wealth-stratification exercise. Only five per cent of farmers in Dangara Salata and Dangara Medalcho PAs were estimated to have a pair of oxen for traction, and 45 per cent of farmers have no livestock of any kind and use hand tools for cultivation. Hand tools are not efficient for digging out weeds, and the prices of these implements are rising all the time.

Farmers without oxen either exchange two days' labour for use of one pair of oxen from a neighbour, or rent their lands to share-croppers, or use mutual work groups (*Debbo*) to work with hand tools on a number of land-holdings on a rota basis.

Wealth stratification

The community groups set three criteria for wealth stratification: oxen, livestock, and land size. On this basis, households in the two PAs were categorised into three groups.

Rich households comprised five per cent of all the households of the area. They own a pair of oxen, a pair of cows, and three *timad* of land (one *timad* = one-fifth of a hectare). Middle-ranked households own an ox for share, a cow to share, a donkey to share, and one *timad* of land. Fifty per cent of the households in the PAs were judged to be in this category.

Poor households had no livestock and no farm land, except for a homestead and 'garden' plot. Forty-five per cent of all households in the PAs fell into this category.

Health problems

Various communicable diseases were mentioned as having a major effect on people's health. It was indicated that typhoid fever,

diarrhoea, amoebic dysentery, pneumonia, and malaria were common. Traditional practices common in the area are female circumcision (that is, female genital mutilation), cutting of the uvula (an extension of the soft palate, above the throat), and tooth extraction.

Malnutrition and diarrhoea were the main diseases affecting infants. The disease calendar which was produced by women's groups also included scabies, respiratory infections, and dysentery. The women participating in discussions understood the significance of inadequate household and environmental hygiene, poor sanitation, and limited diet as causes of these diseases.

Most people in the PAs want to use modern health services when they fall sick, but the closest clinic is at Areka, about two hours' walk away. In addition, people could not afford the high cost of drugs.

Mother and child health care

Mothers usually deliver at home with the help of friends and relatives. It is only when they face a prolonged labour, or complications are expected, that the Trained Traditional Birth Attendant (TTBA) is called. There is only one TTBA for both Dangara Salata and Dangara Madelcho PAs.

During discussions about health, most of the women's group (10 out of 15 members) said that they did not attend ante-natal services. The distance to Areka Health Centre was the main reason. Few women knew much about family-planning services; and most want to have more children, primarily to replace those who died in infancy.

Women's groups stressed the problems of fetching water from the river, which is some distance from most villages in the PAs. Grinding was also mentioned as a heavy part of their workload.

Problem ranking and analysis

After collating ranked problems from men's and women's groups in Dangara Salata and Dangara Madelcho PAs, it was clear that clean water (17 points), a health clinic (15 points), and fertiliser (13 points) were the priority needs.

Analysing the ranking by gender, we found that the women's priorities were associated with their heaviest work: fetching water and grinding. An accessible health institution was also a priority. The men's groups felt that water and health were major problems, after fertiliser.

• Both PA communities fetch water from the Alolla river, which is contaminated and a long distance from most villages. Many of the common diseases could be minimised by the provision of safe drinking water.

• The clinic at Areka town is too far away for mothers, children, the elderly, and sick people, so strengthening local MCH services and health-education programmes was seen as a real priority.

• Installing a grinding mill for the two PAs (and possibly for neighbouring PAs as well) could reduce women's work in processing food, but it was recognised that this would be a major capital input.

• The high price of fertiliser was not easy to address, as there is no strong local institution which could supply it, or run a credit and loan scheme to assist the farmers.

Conclusion

The diagnostic survey undertaken with Dubbo Catholic Mission is an example of how the determinant factors of development in a particular locality can be pinpointed through the use of diagnostic techniques.

The Dubbo Mission MCH team made the following comment concerning the diagnostic survey exercise in the two PAs in their Annual Report of 30 April 1994:

Based on the results of this survey, we realised the greatest needs of the people — a safe and adequate water supply and a health facility, as they were completely deprived of both.

A Health Committee at Dangara Salata was formed on 19 January 1994, which was chaired by the Head of the Wereda Health Office. On 1 February 1994 a meeting was held with the Regional Administrator on the [needs of] the local community at the Dangara Salata site. They [the community] have worked and repaired the most dangerous parts of the roads leading into the area. Also the Dubbo Mission Fathers have repaired the bridge and made it safe for us. The Health Committee provided a large and spacious tukul [local thatched house] for our work.

Communities are dynamic, and development programmes must reflect this dynamism. Only by this means can development workers hope to make a lasting improvement in the quality of life of the community with whom they are working.

The authors

Yezichalem Kassa is the Health Adviser and Feleke Tadele the Community Development Officer in the Programme Support Unit (PSU) of Oxfam UK/I's Addis Ababa Office. The PSU is involved in all aspects of the development activities undertaken within Oxfam's programme in Ethiopia and provides advice, training, and support where necessary.

This article first appeared in *Development in Practice*, Volume 5, Number 3, in 1995.

Empowerment examined

Jo Rowlands

Power and empowerment

The often uncritical use of the term 'empowerment' in development thinking and practice disguises a problematic concept. Many development practitioners and policy-makers will have come across the term in Caroline Moser's work (1989) on gender analysis. However, development is not the only context in which it is used. We now hear about empowerment from mainstream politicians such as Bill Clinton and John Major. Its use in some disciplines — adult education, community work, and social work in particular — is relatively advanced, though here too there is room for greater clarity about the concept and its application.

Some of the confusion arises because the root-concept — power — is itself disputed, and so is understood and experienced in differing ways by different people. Indeed, the person invoking 'empowerment' may not even be aware of the potential for misunderstanding. Power has been the subject of much debate across the social sciences.[1] Some definitions focus, with varying degrees of subtlety, on the availability of one person or group to get another person or group to do something against their will. Such 'power' is located in decision-making processes, conflict, and force, and could be described as 'zero-sum': the more power one person has, the less the other has. Other definitions differentiate between various kinds of power, which can then be understood as serving distinct purposes and having different effects in or on society. These include 'a threat power', 'economic power', and 'integrative power'; or 'the power to create such relationships as love, respect, friendship, legitimacy and so on'.[2]

Most frameworks for understanding power appear to be 'neutral': that is, they make no mention of how power is *actually* distributed within a society. There is no consideration of the power dynamics of gender, or of race, class, or any other force of oppression. This absence is tackled by a number of feminist theorists.[3] Conventionally, power is defined in relation to obedience, or 'power over', since some people are seen to have control or influence over others. A gender analysis shows that 'power over' is wielded predominantly by men over other men, by men over women, and by dominant social, political, economic, or cultural groups over those who are marginalised. It is thus an instrument of domination, whose use can be seen in people's personal lives, their close relationships, their communities, and beyond.

Power of this kind can be subtly exercised. Various feminist writers have described the way in which people who are systematically denied power and influence in the dominant society internalise the messages they receive about what they are supposed to be like, and how they may come to believe the messages to be true.[4] This 'internalised oppression' is adopted as a survival mechanism, but becomes so well ingrained that the effects are mistaken for reality. Thus, for example, a woman who is subjected to violent abuse when she expresses her own opinions may start to withhold them, and eventually come to believe that she has no opinions of her own. When control becomes internalised in this way, the overt use of 'power over' is no longer necessary.

The definition of power in terms of domination and obedience contrasts with one which views it in generative terms: for instance 'the power some people have of stimulating activity in others and raising their morale'.[5] One aspect of this is the kind of leadership that comes from the wish to see a group achieve what it is capable of, where there is no conflict of interests and the group sets its own collective agenda. This model of power is not a zero-sum: an increase in one person's power does not necessarily diminish that of another. And, as Liz Kelly (1992) observes, 'I suspect it is "power to" that the term "empowerment" refers to, and it is achieved by increasing one's ability to resist and challenge "power over".'

What is empowerment?

The meaning of 'empowerment' can now be seen to relate to the user's interpretation of power. In the context of the conventional definition, empowerment must be about bringing people who are outside the decision-making process into it. This puts a strong emphasis on access to political structures and formal decision-making and, in the economic sphere, on access to markets and incomes that enable people to participate in economic decision-making. It is about individuals being able to maximise the opportunities available to them without or despite constraints of structure and State. Within the generative interpretation of power, empowerment also includes access to intangible decision-making processes. It is concerned with the processes by which people become aware of their own interests and how these relate to those of others, in order to participate from a position of greater strength in decision-making and actually to influence such decisions.

Feminist interpretations of power lead to a still broader understanding of empowerment, since they go beyond formal and institutional definitions of power, and incorporate the idea of 'the personal as political'.[6] From a feminist perspective, interpreting 'power over' entails understanding the dynamics of oppression and internalised oppression. Since these affect the ability of less powerful groups to participate in formal and informal decision-making, and to exert influence, they also affect the way that individuals or groups perceive themselves and their ability to act and influence the world around them. Empowerment is thus more than simply opening up access to decision-making; it must also include the processes that lead people to perceive themselves as able and entitled to occupy that decision-making space, and so overlaps with the other categories of 'power to' and 'power from within'.

These interpretations of empowerment involve giving full scope to the full range of human abilities and potential. As feminist and other social theorists have shown, the abilities ascribed to a particular set of people are to a large degree socially constructed. Empowerment must involve undoing negative social constructions, so that the people affected come to see themselves as having the capacity and the right to act and have influence.

This wider picture of empowerment can be seen to have three dimensions:

- **Personal:** where empowerment is about developing a sense of self and individual confidence and capacity, and undoing the effects of internalised oppression.

- **Close relationships:** where empowerment is about developing the ability to negotiate and influence the nature of the relationship and decisions made within it.

- **Collective:** where individuals work together to achieve a more extensive impact than each could have had alone. This includes involvement in political structures, but might also cover collective action based on cooperation rather than competition. Collective action may be locally focused — for example, at village or neighbourhood level

— or institutional, such as national networks or the United Nations.

The profound — but often unrecognised — differences in the ways in which power is understood perhaps explain how it is that people and organisations as far apart politically as feminists, Western politicians, and the World Bank have embraced the concept with such enthusiasm.

Empowerment in practice

The idea of empowerment is increasingly used as a tool for understanding what is needed to change the situation of poor and marginalised people. In this context, there is broad agreement that empowerment is a process; that it involves some degree of personal development, but that this is not sufficient; and that it involves moving from insight to action.

In a counselling context, McWhirter (1991) defines empowerment as:

*The **process** by which people, organisations or groups who are powerless (a) become aware of the power dynamics at work in their life context, (b) develop the skills and capacity for gaining some reasonable control over their lives, (c) exercise this control without infringing upon the rights of others and (d) support the empowerment of others in the community.* (my emphasis)

She makes a useful distinction between 'the situation of empowerment', where all four of these conditions are met; and 'an empowering situation', where one or more of the conditions is in place or being developed, but where the full requirements are not present.

Through all these definitions runs the theme of understanding: if you understand your situation, you are more likely to act to do something about it. There is also the theme of acting collectively. McWhirter's definition makes clear that taking action is not about gaining the power to dominate others. Writers on social group work also insist that empowerment must be used in the context of oppression, since empowerment is about working to remove the existence and effects of unjust inequalities (Ward and Mullender, 1991). Empowerment can take place on a small scale, linking people with others in similar situations through self-help, education, support, or social action groups and network building; or on a larger scale, through community organisation, campaigning, legislative lobbying, social planning, and policy development (Parsons, 1991).

The definitions of empowerment used in education, counselling, and social work, although developed through work in industrialised countries, are broadly similar to Freire's concept of *conscientisation*, which centres on individuals becoming 'subjects' in their own lives and developing a 'critical consciousness' — that is, an understanding of their circumstances and the social environment that leads to action.

In practice, much empowerment work involves forms of group work. The role of the outside professional in this context becomes one of helper and facilitator; anything more directive is seen as interfering with the empowerment of the people concerned. Since facilitation skills require subtlety in order to be effective, this has usually meant that professionals must to some extent re-learn how to do their jobs, and develop high-level skills of self-awareness. In some cases, the professional facilitator has to become a member of the group, and be willing to do the same kind of personal sharing as is encouraged from other participants.

The outside professional cannot expect to control the outcomes of authentic empowerment. Writing about education, Taliaferro (1991) points out that true power cannot be bestowed: it comes from within. Any notion of empowerment being given by one group or another hides an attempt to keep control, and she describes the idea of gradual empowerment as 'especially dubious'. Real empowerment may take unanticipated directions. Outside professionals should therefore be clear that any 'power over' which they have in relation to the people they work with is likely to be challenged by them. This raises an ethical and political issue: if the reality is that you *do* have 'power over' — as is the case with statutory authorities or financially powerful organisations, such as development agencies — it is misleading to deny that this is so.

Empowerment in a development context

How can the concept of empowerment be most usefully applied in a development context? Most of the literature about empowerment, with the exception of Freire and Batliwala, originates from work in industrialised societies. Do poor or otherwise marginalised women and men experience similar problems in developing countries? In both cases, their lack of access to resources and to formal power is significant, even if the contexts within which that lack is experienced are very different. McWhirter's definition of empowerment seems equally relevant to either context. Any difference is more likely to show up in the way in which it is put into practice, and in the particular activities that are called for. This is confirmed in one of the few definitions of empowerment which has a specific focus on development (Keller and Mbwewe, 1991), in which it is described as:

A process whereby women become able to organise themselves to increase their own self-reliance, to assert their independent right to make choices and to control resources which will assist in challenging and eliminating their own subordination.

Srilatha Batliwala, writing about women's empowerment, has made a detailed analysis of women's empowerment programmes, looking at Integrated Rural Development (IRD: economic interventions, awareness-building, and organising of women) and at Research, Training, and Resource Support.[7] She notes that in some (especially IRD) programmes, the terms *empowerment* and *development* are used

synonymously. It is often assumed that power comes automatically through economic strength. It may do, but often it does not, depending on specific relations determined by gender, culture, class, or caste. Economic relations do not always improve women's economic situation, and often add an extra burden. Often, development work is still done 'for' women, and an exclusive focus on economic activities does not automatically create a space for women to look at their own role *as women*, or at other problematic aspects of their lives.

Economic activities and the empowerment process

Economic activities may widen the range of options for marginalised people, but do not necessarily enable them to reach a point where they can take charge of creating for themselves the options from which they get to choose. To do that, a combination of confidence and self-esteem, information, analytical skills, ability to identify and tap into available resources, political and social influence, and so on, is needed. Programmes that build on the demands and wishes of the people who participate in them are a step towards empowerment, but they do not in and of themselves tackle the assumptions that those people (and the people around them) are already making about what they can and cannot do: the point where the internalised oppression works in combination with the particular economic and social context to restrict the options that people *perceive* as available, and legitimate. An empowerment approach centred on economic activity must pay attention to more than the activity itself. The processes and structures through which an economic activity operates need to be deliberately designed to create opportunities for an empowerment process to happen.

The role of outsiders

The role of the professional or the outsider in the development setting is just as important as in the social-work contexts described earlier.

Price describes the crucial role played by women staff of an Indian NGO, giving an example of an occasion when a key worker talking about her own personal experience enabled other women to do likewise. This is in stark contrast to the tendency in many development projects, as in Ngau's account (1987) of the Kenyan Harambee movement, for professional–client relationships to be fostered by para-professionals, fuelling resentment and withdrawal among local people. This has implications for the way in which personnel in development programmes and projects — as well as in aid agencies — perform their work. A process of empowerment that seeks to engage poor and marginalised people cannot be effective if the methodology is 'top–down' and directive, or encourages dependency. Empowerment is a process that cannot be imposed by outsiders — although appropriate external support and intervention can speed up and encourage it. It calls for a facilitative approach and an attitude of complete respect for and confidence in the people being worked with, or accompanied.[8] It therefore makes great demands on the change-agents, and may require (and feed into) their own empowerment. Furthermore, since most professionals are trained to work in ways that disempower — and which tell other people what they should do and think — it requires conscious and sustained efforts to modify that pattern of behaviour and to clarify mutual expectations.

Individual empowerment

In discussing empowerment through awareness-building and organising of women, Batliwala highlights an aspect of an empowerment approach that poses a difficulty for many agencies working in development: it can be desperately slow. Most funding agencies are understandably preoccupied with showing results. Yet the work needed for raising levels of confidence and self-esteem among poor and marginalised people in such a way that will enhance their ability to take charge of their own needs is necessarily time-consuming. It is a process for each individual to do at her or his own pace. Because of this, there is a temptation to work with people who have already a degree of self-confidence. This is one reason why even empowerment-focused programmes often fail to engage with the poorest and most marginalised. Even to participate in a group, you require a certain minimal sense of your own abilities and worth, as well as being able to overcome the obstacles to making the time to participate.

Collective empowerment

In the context of development, while individual empowerment is one ingredient in achieving empowerment at the collective and institutional levels, concentration on individuals alone is not enough. Changes are needed in the collective abilities of individuals to take charge of identifying and meeting their own needs — as households, communities, organisations, institutions, and societies. At the same time, we must recognise that the effectiveness of such group activity rests also on the individual empowerment of at least some people.

Professionals involved in such empowerment work should repeatedly ask how the development intervention is affecting the various aspects of the lives of the people directly involved. A monitoring and evaluation process that reflects the empowerment process is essential. People need to be involved in the identification of appropriate indicators of change, and in the setting of criteria for evaluating impact. As the empowerment process proceeds, these will inevitably need to be modified and revised. Clarity about the dynamics that push poor and marginalised people to stay within what is safe and familiar is vital, in order to ensure that the empowerment process is kept well in focus. Qualitative indicators are, self-evidently, central to the evaluation of empowerment.

Conclusion

'Empowerment' has much in common with other concepts used by development practitioners and planners, such as 'participation', 'capacity-building', 'sustainability', or 'institutional development'. There is, however, a worrying temptation to use them in a way that takes the troublesome notions of power, and the distribution of power, out of the picture. For in spite of their appeal, these terms can easily become one more way to ignore or hide the realities of power, inequality, and oppression. Yet it is precisely those realities which shape the lives of poor and marginalised people, and the communities in which they live.

The concept of 'empowerment', if it is used precisely and deliberately, can help to focus thought, planning, and action in development. However, when its use is careless, deliberately vague, or sloganising, it risks becoming degraded and valueless.

Notes

1 See, for example, Bachrach and Baratz (1970), Lukes (1974), Foucault (1980), Giddens (1984), Hartsock (1985 and 1990), and Boulding (1988).

2 These distinctions are from Boulding (1988) p.10.

3 See, for example, Hartsock (1985, 1990), and Starhawk (1987).

4 See, for example, Pheterson (1990), and Jackins (1983).

5 Nancy Hartsock (1985) draws on the writings of Hannah Arendt, Mary Parker Follett, Dorothy Emmett, Hannah Pitkin and Berenice Carroll in her analysis.

6 I do not wish to imply here that there is one 'feminist' model of power. Space constraints have led me to generalise and leave out important variations in analysis.

7 Batliwala (1993). I had access to the second draft and not to the final version.

8 *Acompañamiento*, or accompaniment, is a word widely used in Latin America to describe an outside agent's sense of solidarity and willingness to share risks with poor and marginalised people, and a willingness to engage with the processes of social change in which they are directly involved. It contrasts with the position of outside agents — whether these are church workers, development NGOs, or funding agencies — which maintain a greater sense of distance.

References

Bachrach, P. and M.S. Baratz (1970) *Power and Poverty: Theory and Practice*, New York: Oxford University Press.

Batliwala, S. (1993) *Empowerment of Women in South Asia: Concepts and Practices*, New Delhi: Asian-South Pacific Bureau of Adult Education and Freedom from Hunger Campaign.

Boulding, K. (1988) *Three Faces of Power*, London: Sage.

Foucault, M. (1980) *Power/Knowledge: Selected Interviews and Other Writings*, ed. Colin Gordon, Brighton: Harvester.

Giddens, A. (1984) *The Constitution of Society*, Cambridge: Polity.

Hartsock, N. (1985) *Money, Sex and Power: Towards a Feminist Historical Materialism*, Boston: Northeastern University Press.

Hartsock, N. (1990) 'Foucault on power: a theory for women?' in L.J. Nicholson, (ed): *Feminism/Postmodernism*, New York and London: Routledge.

Jackins, H. (1983) *The Reclaiming of Power*, Seattle: Rational Island.

Keller, B. and D.C. Mbwewe (1991) 'Policy and planning for the empowerment of Zambia's women farmers', *Canadian Journal of Development Studies* 12/1: 75-88.

Kelly, L. (1992) 'The Contradictions of Power for Women', paper presented at the NFHA Women and Housing Conference. Mimeo.

Lukes, S. (1974) *Power: a Radical View*, London: Macmillan.

McWhirter, E.H. (1991) 'Empowerment in

counselling', *Journal of Counselling and Development* 69: 222-7.

Moser, C. (1989) 'Gender planning in the Third World: meeting practical and strategic gender needs', *World Development*, 17:11.

Ngau, P.M. (1987) 'Tensions in empowerment: the experience of Harambee (self-help) movement, Kenya', *Economic Development and Cultural Change* 35/3:523-8.

Parsons, R.J. (1991) 'Empowerment: purpose and practice principle in social work', *Social Work with Groups* 14/2:7-21

Pheterson, G. (1990) 'Alliances between women: overcoming internalised oppression and internalised domination' in A. Albrecht and R.M. Brewer (eds): *Bridges of Power: Women's Multicultural Alliances*, Philadelphia: New Society.

Price, J. (n.d.) 'Women's Development: Welfare Projects or Political Empowerment?', presented at Amsterdam conference. Mimeo.

Starhawk [pseud. M. Simos] (1987) *Truth or Dare: Encounters with Power, Authority and Mystery*, San Francisco: Harper & Row.

Taliaferro, M.B. (1991) 'The myth of empowerment', *Journal of Negro Education* 60/1: 1-2.

Ward, D. and A. Mullender (1991) 'Empowerment and oppression: an indissoluble pairing', *Critical Social Policy* 11/2:21-30.

The author

Jo Rowlands has worked for over ten years as a trainer and consultant for cooperatives and NGOs in Britain and Latin America. She is Co-director of Manantial Women's International Link, a British NGO that brings together women from industrialised and developing countries.

This article first appeared in *Development in Practice* Volume 5, Number 2, in 1995.

Some thoughts on gender and culture

Maitrayee Mukhopadhyay

In an article which appeared in *Development in Practice*, Volume 5, Number 3, Mike Powell raised many issues about subjective perceptions, mainly those of 'outsiders' who interfere in cultures they do not fully understand. Such dilemmas have implications for 'insiders' as well as 'outsiders', because all practitioners are in some way intervening in processes of social transformation, and are involved in the business of allocating resources.

I want to explore the issue of gender and culture: areas where the ways in which development practitioners understand and intervene in a situation can further entrench gender-based inequality, or demonstrate the possibility that such inequalities are open to challenge.

In India, I operate within my own society and culture, and so am an 'insider'. But in my work for gender equity, I have often experienced allegations from different quarters that this is against our culture, violates our traditions, and (the worst criticism of all in the Indian context) that it is 'Westernised'. It is common for gender and development practitioners to be labelled in this manner, though the precise allegations may differ from one place to another. Gender relations are viewed as among the most intimate aspects of our cultural traditions, and challenging them seems to challenge the very basis of who we are.

In 1984, I published a book about women and development in India, and undertook a publicity tour in the United Kingdom. Among many presentations I made, the most memorable for me was at the Pakistan Centre in Liverpool. Most of the predominantly male audience were from India, Pakistan, or Bangladesh.

The discussion that followed my talk was lively, to say the least, and abusive at its worst. My book criticised the Indian model of development for working against women's interests, and Indian society for its treatment of women. I was initially taken aback by the reaction, until it dawned on me what was happening. The Indians, Pakistanis, and Bangladeshis had united (leaving aside, for the time being, their bitter differences on the sub-continent) in a vigorous defence of culture and tradition: a tradition which respected its women, a tradition which was protective of its women, and one in which women were the centre of families which, in turn, were collectivities of co-operation, love, and sacrifice. In fact, they were drawing a simplified picture of gender relations which amounted to a fiction of a monolithic, timeless culture: an immutable, 'South Asian' culture.

I had offended my audience, first by 'turning traitor' to my own culture, and raising doubts about women's position in Indian society. Secondly, I had done so in a Western country which they had decided to perceive, in the interests of preserving their own separate cultural identity, as a culture full of 'loose' women, and broken families.

There was a sequel to this experience: a Pakistani woman followed me out of the hall, and thanked me for my presentation. She had been working with Asian women facing domestic violence, ever since her daughter committed suicide, unable to endure further harassment and torture in her marital home.

I am often asked, usually by expatriate development workers, whether by intervening on women's behalf we are upsetting the gender roles and relations characteristic of the culture. The fear that we may be imposing our own cultural values by promoting gender equity in our development work is a real one. However, it is real largely *because* we allow our own culture-based assumptions about women to colour our response to alternative visions of gender equality. And we fail to recognise the everyday forms of resistance put up by subordinated groups, because these do not correspond to our experience.

If gender relations are equated with the most intimate aspects of our cultures, and if culture and tradition are assumed to be immutable, rather than the site of resistance from subordinated groups, gender relations soon become a 'no-go area'; and allocating resources in order to redress the imbalance of power between men and women is made politically difficult.

But cultures are not fixed or immutable. Contests to 'fix' the meanings of social entities take place all the time, leading to changes in social practices. Development practitioners have to take sides in those contests which help to dismantle hierarchies of gender and class. By failing to recognise that these are going on, and listening only to the voice of the powerful in society, we are in fact taking the side of the fundamentalists, who render religion uniform throughout the world by enforcing traditions of hierarchical gender roles and relations, and presenting them as unchanging and authoritative.

There are no hard and fast distinctions between the material world and the world of ideas, values, and beliefs. We must work at both levels to bring about the changes that are supposed to be the purpose of development. I end with a plea for development practitioners to use culture as a way to open up intractable areas of gender relations, and not to regard it as a dead end which prevents us from working towards more equitable relations between women and men.

The author

Maitrayee Mukhopadhyay is a Gender and Development Adviser for Oxfam (UK and Ireland), focusing on South Asia and the Middle East. Her book, *Silver Shackles*, was published by Oxfam (UK and Ireland) in 1984.

This article first appeared in *Development in Practice*, Volume 5, Number 4 (1995). The ideas in it are developed more fully in a paper by the author, published in *Gender and Development*, Volume 3, Number 1, pp. 13-18.

Who is the expert?

Valerie Emblen

Advisers: part of the problem, or part of the solution?

In 1990, I flew to Lao People's Democratic Republic (Lao PDR) to work as Pre-school Adviser to the Ministry of Education. It was my first time on extended work overseas. The Ministry of Education had asked for help in developing teaching methodology in kindergartens and training colleges for pre-school teachers. The project was planned and supported by the Save the Children Fund (SCF/UK). When I arrived, I discovered that the Ministry expected me to write training manuals, which they would translate into Lao, and then we would set up training courses on how to use them. I had never had to consider how to 'package' teaching methods, or even if there were any 'proper' teaching methods that everyone should know. Above all, I was concerned about the relevance of my English knowledge in this very different context. I had an uncomfortable few months while I re-negotiated my role, all the time aware that I was not the adviser that was expected.

In the Lao language, *seosan* means adviser or expert; the word conveys a general respect for learning. Both words, *seosan* and *expert*, convey the notion that a person can possess valuable knowledge that is independent of any particular context. Those trying to develop an education system may well believe that there is something that they don't know, some secret that they lack, which is hampering their development. I saw how, in an under-confident system, people are tempted to search for the magic answer: the methods and materials that are perfectly teacher-proofed. This is a delusion, but the myth seems to be promoted by governments and funders alike.

I was the latest in a long line of advisers to the Teacher Training Department: in the previous ten years they had had a Russian, a Cuban, and Vietnamese. I discovered only after a long time in Laos that there was a very ambivalent attitude to foreign advisers. I heard comments like: 'They get paid huge salaries and we have to do the work' ... 'We had to rewrite the project completely after they went' ... 'They don't know about our country: they've never been outside Vientiane, what do they know?' NGO advisers don't escape scepticism, and there was the feeling that they are not always very well qualified: 'Advisers should have real expertise in their *own* countries.'

Attitudes to new projects are ambivalent: they are started with high hopes and often unrealistic expectations, while, at the same time, years of failure have made people sceptical about the possibility of success. They can be defensive and unwilling to commit themselves in case of another failure. But advisers keep coming, and each new one represents a new start, while previous work is swept away. The stream of advisers has had the effect of disempowering local teachers. Curriculum documents are glossier now that the Eastern bloc experts have left and Western organisations have taken their place, but they are beginning to stack up high, the edges turning yellow. Meanwhile, children still go to school without books, and teachers go on teaching until the last bit of chalk is used up and, two years behind in their salary, they go back to work in their fields.

I have had constantly to remind myself that advisers can be the problem as well as the solution. Simply transferring knowledge from one place to another will not help, as was made clear to me one day when I was approached by a Lao teacher trainer who taught the Child Health Course. She asked me if we really feed babies with big spoons in Europe and, 'If so, how do you do it?' Her teaching material, written by the Russian adviser, said 'Take three table-spoons of ...' and she had never used table-spoons as measures. She is an intelligent, professional person, and the story shows how it is possible to get people to mistrust their own commonsense knowledge.

In Vientiane, it is all too common for foreign developers to express poor opinions of their Lao colleagues. One Ministry official felt the need to start a discussion with the comment: 'I don't know if you know, but not everyone in Lao Ministries is lazy.' An NGO's report on its work in Indo-China argues that more than usual numbers of expatriate advisers are needed, because of 'low-calibre counterparts' (SCF 1992). A myth is being built that 'under-development' (whatever that may be) is caused by gaps in skill and understanding, and that those gaps can be plugged by bringing in people from places where they know more: a simplistic analysis, which allows us to avoid much more difficult issues of respect, equality, and justice. Fortunately, my work in London had made me aware of the ways in which negative views of other cultures are generated.

Social reality and cross-cultural communication

Interventions are designed to bring about changes, but changes do not happen in a vacuum: they have an impact on people's lives. Soon after I arrived, the head-teacher of the Dong Dok kindergarten, who had been supported and trained by SCF (UK), was unceremoniously removed from her post by the Dong Dok Teacher Training School. They felt that preference had been given to her over more senior people; she had been sent on training courses, and had been given a motorbike. The last straw was when her husband was seen riding the bike to town. It seemed a trivial incident and, from the outside, an unreasonable and bizarrely self-destructive decision. But this is the reality in which people live and work. Foreign advisers can be very egocentric, and fail to see that their work is located in a social context; power games, jealousies, and battles to maintain status are common everywhere. Difficulties for foreign advisers are magnified, because they are not a part of the cultural context and do not understand the social dynamics. Ignorance is not blame-worthy, but lack of sensitivity to the importance of social meanings is.

Lao PDR is a non-confrontational society, and politeness demands that advisers are not contradicted. Many outsiders are frustrated by the fact that apparently agreed actions do not go ahead; but the Lao people have developed techniques which allow them to make their views known subtly, without overtly challenging the adviser. They will avoid doing things they think inappropriate; foreigners then accuse them of being lazy or lacking interest. And the frustration is two-way. I also know that my style of communicating (I seldom answer questions directly) caused problems. For example, a Ministry colleague quite uncharacteristically burst out at a meeting: 'The adviser won't tell us all she knows.' I had to recognise that neither side would fully understand the other's communication style in the short space of a two-year contract, but we could learn to minimise the importance of misunderstandings and to laugh at them.

Cross-cultural communication is challenging, but I don't want to exaggerate its difficulty: we all have resources of human knowledge and empathy to draw on. Most importantly, I have seen how easy it is, when you misunderstand others' intentions, to attribute poor motives to them.

Addressing the issues and taking risks

A Lao colleague quoted a proverb to me: *You showed us how to prepare the fish, but you didn't cook it for us.* She was comment-ing on the ways we had worked together. We, Lao counterparts and I, had to plan a way to initiate change. During this time in Lao PDR, I had to accept that some of my fundamental beliefs were, in fact, the product of a Western conventional wisdom. Counterparts also had their own cherished beliefs and conventional wisdom. To illustrate differences in perceptions, I quote from the findings of research I am currently undertaking in Lao PDR and England. Teachers of young children are being asked what are the most important things for young children to learn. In England, teachers stressed autonomy, self-expression, and independence, whereas Lao teachers put social values at the top of the list: politeness, caring, and respect for others. The challenge was to listen carefully to what others felt was real and important, without relinquishing the right to suggest other interpretations and possibilities.

In the training colleges, teacher-trainers would teach by reading out the curriculum documents for the students to write in their own notebooks. We set out to find out from the trainers why they did it this way, what sort of teaching methods they wanted to achieve, and what they saw as the constraints. It emerged that they, like all professionals, wanted to develop their teaching, but they felt disempowered by many circumstances, some real and some imaginary. Recently one of the teacher-trainers reminded me that she had argued that students couldn't be allowed to discuss ideas, because 'They are too stupid'. She was happy to admit she had been proved wrong. The trainers said their only teaching aid was the blackboard; they could not always

understand the content of the curriculum; and some said they couldn't allow students to ask questions, because they didn't know the answers themselves. It took a degree of trust to reveal these things. From there, we could identify strengths on which we could build, and plan how to acquire the new knowledge and techniques that were needed. The process was slow and hard for those involved: learning in this mode is not a comfortable process; people are required to commit themselves, to challenge some dearly-held beliefs, and to take risks. Perhaps the reluctance to take risks is the most significant. Governments want certainties: measurable outcomes in measured time-scales, to repay the time and energy they have invested. To want success is normal. But in the effort to ensure it, officials may narrow their focus to leave nothing to chance, with the result that the new is practically indistinguishable from the old.

The processes were agreed with the Ministry and for some time were welcomed, as trainers' and teachers' confidence and competence developed. However, other projects, with much bigger funding, including one financed by the Asian Development Bank, were the responsibility of the Ministry. The Bank employed expatriate 'experts' on six-month contracts, one to write each subject of the Primary Teacher Training Curriculum. They were offering certainties — the correct percentage of theory in proportion to practice, comprehensive lists of teaching methods, proper formats for lesson plans — while the Pre-school Project was still posing questions. I am convinced that our way of working is equally likely to produce long-term change, but the 'experts' had an aura of authority conferred by their international status and, since the Lao government is paying the Bank's advisers astronomically high salaries from loan money, it is quite understandable that their work was accorded high credibility.

We are fortunate that we have had time to show progress and that enough Ministry officials are convinced of the benefits of our way of working that the project will have the opportunity to carry on. What the long-term outcomes will be, I don't know.

The place of overseas advisers

Is there a place for the overseas adviser? I think there is. I have, throughout my career, welcomed help from those with relevant experience. We all need new ideas, new challenges and stimulation; but the way in which the advice is offered is important. I am convinced that outside knowledge should be carefully negotiated and interlinked with local expertise, and that local expertise should be given greater respect.

A story current in Vientiane, which is probably apocryphal, concerns a primary-school science curriculum recently prepared by an Australian adviser which requires a beaker of ice and a thermometer. Mis-matches are seldom so blatant, but bias can be exceedingly powerful. To illustrate this, I quote a passage from a recent survey of Lao children (Phanjarunti 1994) carried out for UNICEF, who are using it to plan their Early Childhood programme:

Overall ... the level of [Lao children's] cognitive development appeared slow at each age — around 76% of the international standard norms. Children cannot tell their age or last name, or know maths concepts (calculating) or colours as they should according to standard norms. Children have slow responses to stimulation.

I suspect that questions more closely related to their lives and interests might have evoked more enthusiastic responses from the children. Sadly, their supposed deficiencies can easily become the focus of programme planning, and the good things which their family and community provide are lost.

Sustainability: desiring and fearing change

Everyone involved in an intervention must hope that it will have a long-lasting impact. If a programme is to bring about long-term change, such change must be deeply rooted. Everyone must really want change, and realistically face the problems involved. In a poor country, financial constraints are an integral part of the work. The system has to be built with what there is. Anything which suggests that change can come about without love, commitment, hard work, and pain is unrealistic. A passionate commitment is needed, for there will be few intrinsic rewards, either in pay and prestige or career prospects. Working with a Ministry where the approach is inevitably 'centre-out' if not 'top down', there is the possibility that change can be brought about quickly; but there is the real possibility of introducing unworkable models if they are not well matched to the reality of the country. Maybe the 'top-down' or 'centre-out' system remains unchallenged because blame can always be passed downwards: the curriculum is good and the methods modern, so problems must lie with the teachers or — worse still — with the students or children.

There is, of course, a tension between the desire for change and the fear of it, but bringing in an outsider is a strong statement about the former. However, the conditions of overseas employment for NGO staff do not always give the security and confidence needed to risk a really developmental approach. Short-term contracts, no proper career structure, poor opportunities for training, and no opportunity to test your own perceptions against those of others undertaking similar contracts can make one feel isolated and unsupported — and that is without all the additional difficulties of being a woman in development work.

I am aware of the many things I failed to resolve; the role of adviser demands a balance between giving people what they ask for and offering alternatives, and I don't know if the balance was right. The group I worked with directly feel good about what they have achieved. On the whole, the Ministry supports the work, though some officials wanted more definite rules and formats. The voices of teachers, parents, and children have been little heard, and they are the most closely affected.

I will not be in Lao PDR in ten years' time to see what remains of what we started, but I loved the experience for the friends I made, and for the opportunity to live in another society and find out how it works. I developed great respect for most of my Lao colleagues, and their ability to develop in the face of many difficulties. The experience has been very challenging. I have been faced with the limits to my own tolerance, my prejudices, and sticking points. I have had, above all, to think about what it is that makes people want to learn and change, and what the role of an outsider can be.

References

Phanjarunti, S., 1994, 'Traditional Child Rearing Practices among Different Ethnic Groups in Houaphan Province, Lao People's Democratic Republic', Vientiane: UNICEF.

Save the Children Fund, 1992, Report of Regional Planning Meeting, January 1992.

The author

After her work in Lao PDR, Valerie Emblen returned to her position as Senior Lecturer in Education at the School of Teaching Studies, University of North London.

This article first appeared in *Development in Practice*, Volume 5, Number 4, in 1995.

Annotated bibliography

This is a selective listing of recent English-language publications relating to social diversity in the context of development and emergency relief work. It was compiled and annotated by Deborah Eade and Caroline Knowles, Editor and Reviews Editor respectively of Development in Practice.

Anderson, Mary B. and P. J. Woodrow:
Rising from the Ashes: Development Strategies in Times of Disaster
Paris: UNESCO//Boulder: Westview Press, 1989
Building on several case-studies, this book shows that relief programmes are never neutral in their developmental impact. It presents a deceptively simple framework for understanding the dynamic relationship between different people's needs, vulnerabilities, and capacities. Analysing most current relief practice, the authors show various practical ways in which it might be improved.

Bangura, Yusuf: *The Search for Identity: Ethnicity, Religion and Political Violence,*
Occasional Paper 6, Geneva: UNRISD, 1994
This paper examines the complex ways in which ethnicity and religion shape social identities, and how people mobilise in support of movements based on such distinctions. It also reflects on the role of violence in social conflicts, on why certain types of violence are preferred by social movements, and on the way in which violence structures the identities of group actors and the dynamics of conflicts. Finally, it examines a range of policy issues relating to the resolution or management of ethnic and religious conflicts, and political violence.

Blaikie, Piers et al.: *At Risk: Natural Hazards, People's Vulnerability and Disasters,*
London: Routledge, 1994

This book reminds the reader that, for most countries, 'natural' disasters are a much more consistent threat than high-profile conflict or 'complex emergencies'. These disasters need not be major — many occur on a local scale — but are just as disruptive to local populations and economies. The other important premise of the book is that the roots of vulnerability to disaster do not lie in the intensity of the hazard solely, but rather in prevailing social and economic conditions *in combination with* the intensity of the hazard. The book usefully models the complex economic and social arrangements and interactions that relate to vulnerability, identifying areas where action to reduce vulnerability can be taken, and presents principles and guidelines to steer this work.

Coleridge, Peter: *Disability, Liberation, and Development,*
Oxford: Oxfam (UK and Ireland), 1993
The situation of disabled people provides a microcosm of the whole development debate and process. Disabled people are oppressed and marginalised in every country of the world, both North and South. Their lives are

constrained by social attitudes which stem from fear and prejudice. By probing these prejudices and studying cases where they have been overcome, we gain an insight into the processes of liberation and empowerment that lie at the heart of any development process. This book provides an overview of the subject and outlines the social, political, and developmental aspects of disability in general terms, illustrating these through case studies from selected countries in Africa, Asia, and the Middle East.

Cook, Rebecca J. (ed.): *Human Rights of Women: National and International Perspectives,*
Philadelphia: University of Pennsylvania Press, 1994
This book asks how human rights can make a difference in the lives of women, given that the very idea of human rights implies universal application to both men and women, across the world. The authors argue that any attempt to address the human rights of women must consider how they can be protected in the context of their own culture and traditions. The book looks at how international human-rights law applies specifically to women in various cultures worldwide, and seeks to develop strategies to promote equitable application of human-rights law at the international, regional, and domestic levels.

Eade, Deborah and Suzanne Williams : *The Oxfam Handbook of Development and Relief,*
Oxford: Oxfam (UK and Ireland), 1995
This three-volume reference book offers a guide to current thinking, policy, and practice in all areas of development and relief work in which Oxfam works in over 70 countries around the world. A central principle is that people's social identities — and hence their perspectives, capacities, and needs — are influenced not only by their economic status, but also by the ways in which social roles are defined in relation to others; and by how society values the individuals comprising it. Chapter Two, 'Focusing on People', explores those aspects of human identity that should

inform all development and relief work. These include gender; ethnic, racial, and cultural identity; childhood and old age; and disability. The practical relevance of these issues is demonstrated in further chapters on Principles of Development and Relief (including Human Rights), Capacity-building (encompassing education and training, as well as advocacy, and institutional development), Production, Health, and Emergencies. A 500-entry annotated Resources Directory comprises the third volume. The Handbook is written for policy-makers, practitioners, and analysts.

Ennew, Judith and Brian Milne : *The Next Generation: Lives of Third World Children,*
London: Zed Books, 1989
This book examines the ways in which children's rights are protected or violated. The first part focuses on the Rights of the Child, featured in the 1989 UN Declaration, and the frequent disparities between policies and their implementation. Inequalities between children in rich and poor nations and in different groups within particular national settings are also considered. The second part of the book comprises a series of 12 case studies, drawing on a wide range of information, and considers the issues raised in the first part.

Gurr, Ted Robert: *Minorities at Risk: A Global View of Ethnopolitical Conflicts,*
Washington: United States Institute of Peace Press, 1993
Possible bases for communal identity include shared historical experiences or myths, religious beliefs, language, ethnicity, region of residence, and, in caste-like systems, customary occupations. The key to identifying such groups is not the presence of a particular trait or set of traits, but the shared perception that these set the group apart. This book surveys over 200 politically active communal groups, with comparative case-studies from Eastern and Western Europe, North Africa and the Middle East, Sub-Saharan Africa, and Japan. Examining their disadvantages and grievances, the author asks: what communal identities and interests are most at odds with the

structures and policies of existing states, and why? Answers may suggest strategies to reduce ethnic conflict, such as autonomy, pluralism, and formal power-sharing.

Jahan, Rounaq
The Elusive Agenda: Mainstreaming Women in Development
London: Zed Books, 1995
This book reviews the progress achieved in making gender a central concern in the development process. It evaluates selected leading bilateral and multilateral donor agencies, including the World Bank, which have played a critical role in shaping the development agenda. It suggests an innovative conceptual framework for analysing Women-in-Development objectives and strategies, and establishing indicators for assessing progress. Policies and measures to promote gender equality and women's advancement are reviewed in a variety of development contexts. The book argues that, in spite of significant advances, the fundamental objective of transforming social and gender relations and creating a more just and equitable world is very far from being achieved. Why has progress been so elusive, for women in particular? It is this question that becomes the central issue explored in this study.

Kabeer, Naila: *Reversed Realities: Gender Hierarchies in Development Thought*
London: Verso Press, 1994
The author traces the emergence of 'women' as a specific category in development thought and examines alternative frameworks for analysing gender hierarchies. The household is identified as a primary site for the construction of power relations and compares the extent to which gender inequalities are revealed in different approaches to the concept of the family unit. The inadequacies of the poverty line as a measuring tool are assessed, and an overview of the issue of population policies is given.

Korten, David C.: *When Corporations Rule the World*
London: Earthscan, 1995

This book documents the human and environmental consequences of globalisation. The globalisation of economic activity has hugely increased the profits and power of multi-national corporations and financial institutions which have superseded old institutional structures based on the dominance of nation states. Rootless and largely unregulated, they are free to pursue their financial aims regardless of the consequences for society. The author also examines why, and how, people all over the world are acting to reclaim their political and economic power from these forces, and he presents a policy agenda for restoring democracy and rooting economic power in people and communities.

Miller, Marc S.: *State of the Peoples: A global human rights report on societies in danger,*
Boston: Beacon Press, 1993
A resource book listing hundreds of indigenous peoples, listed by geographical region, together with articles on the critical issues facing different indigenous peoples, especially human rights and environmental concerns. Compiled by Survival International, a research group based in the USA.

Moghadam, Valentine: *Identity, Politics and Women: Cultural Reassertions and Feminism in Perspective*
Boulder: Westview, 1994
'Identity politics' refers to questions of religious, ethnic, and national identity. This book looks at political-cultural movements that are m aking a bid for state power, for fundamental judicial change, or for cultural hegemony. In particular, the contributors explore the relations of culture, identity, and women, providing vivid illustrations from around the world of the compelling nature of Woman as a cultural symbol and Woman as a political pawn in male-directed power struggles. The discussions also provide evidence of women as active participants and active opponents of such movements. The book offers theoretical, comparative, and historical approaches to the study of identity

politics, together with 13 case-studies spanning Christian, Hindu, Jewish, and Muslim countries and communities.

Moody, Roger: *The Indigenous Voice: Visions and Realities*
London, Zed Books, 1998
A reader in two volumes containing hundreds of testimonies from indigenous peoples (mainly from North and South America, and Australasia), providing an overview of the issues which they face, such as invasion, genocide, militarisation, mining and multi-nationals, pollution, tourism, and racism.

Sen, Amartya: *Inequality Re-examined*
Oxford: Oxford University Press, 1992
A monograph in which Sen poses philo-sophical and moral questions about the notion of equality and inequality. He suggests that the wish for equality is common to virtually all theories of social ethics, but considers that the central question is 'equality of *what*?'. The importance of this question derives from the diversity of human beings: our individual characteristics (such as age, sex, general abilities, particular talents), as well as our circumstances (social backgrounds, ownership of assets, environmental predicaments, and so on). Diversity, he argues, is no secondary factor to be ignored, or introduced ('later on'): it is a fundamental aspect of our interest in equality. Contains an extensive and impressive bibliography.

Sen, Gita and Caren.Grown: *Development Crises and Alternative Visions*
DAWN, 1987
A brief introduction to development econ-omics, written from a Southern feminist perspective, which examines why strategies designed to achieve overall economic growth and increased industrial and agricultural prod-uctivity have proven to be harmful to women. The authors argue that many long-term economic processes have been indifferent (if not damaging) to the interests and needs of poor people in general, and women in particular. Women's contributions are central to the ability of households, communities, and nations to survive, and a much-needed reorientation of developent analysis can be achieved by starting from the perspective of poor women. The authors also emphasise the diversity which exists among women, and argue that it is necessary and legitimate to define feminism so that it includes the struggle against all forms of oppression.

Stavenhagen, Rodolfo: *The Ethnic Question: Conflicts, Development, and Human Rights*
Tokyo: UN University Press, 1990
This book presents a comprehensive picture of contemporary ethnic issues as manifested in most of the world's major regions. Following a discussion of ethnic issues in relation to the theories of nation, State, modernisation processes, and class, and from the point of view of several social science approaches, the case of Latin America is presented as an example of the preceding theoretical considerations. The author also examines the extent of ethnic-rights protection in the United Nations and other international systems: the special problems of indigenous and tribal peoples, increasing racism in Western Europe, and, finally, the cultural and educational policies of govern-ments in relation to ethnic minorities.

Stiefel, Matthias and Marshall Wolfe: *A Voice for the Excluded: Popular Participation in Development —Utopia or Necessity?*
London: Zed Books/UNRISD, 1994
Participation, like sustainable development, has become a catchword — widely advocated, seldom defined, and rarely put into practice. After reviewing various conceptions of participation, this book pulls together the findings of original field studies. In addition to focusing on the organised efforts of the 'excluded', it analyses other relevant actors — NGOs, the State, and international agencies — as they encourage, co-opt, or undermine participatory struggles and initiatives.

Tinker, Irene (ed.): *Persistent Inequalities: Women and World Development*
Oxford: Oxford University Press, 1990
This collection of essays introduces the field of women in development and offers an overview of debates that have challenged many earlier assumptions about development and the reality of women's work and lives within and outside the household. In addition, the book shows the connection with the global women's movement and the impact of these advocates and new scholarship on the policies and management of development policies. The authors come from both developed and developing countries; among them are practitioners, development economists, and feminist scholars — and each one has in a different way addressed the question that runs throughout: why do inequalities persist?

Tout, Ken: *Ageing in Developing Countries*
Oxford: Oxford University Press with HelpAge International, 1989
This book aims to set out the available facts about forecast increases in longevity and to present a positive view, based on a number of pilot programmes, of the ways in which potential problems associated with ageing can be met. It therefore proposes a new approach to the problems of older people in developing countries: the intention is to build structures for the future, which means stimulating awareness of this incipient but rapidly developing problem, and providing local communities with the resources to take their own actions. The author also stresses the importance of mobilising and maximising the many talents and the wealth of experience of elderly people themselves into productive programmes.

Tout, Ken: *Elderly Care: A World Perspective*
London: Chapman and Hall, 1993
At a time when the population of almost every country is ageing rapidly, new approaches are called for to meet the problems of caring for the elderly. Many older people can no longer depend on extended family support. This is a problem of current concern in industrialised countries, and the same trend is now evident in developing countries. The essays in this book give examples of ageing programmes from all over the world, with studies from nearly 40 countries, covering a wide range of subjects including care at home, community support, elders' empowerment, elder participation, income generation, environment, and women's ageing.

UN Centre for Human Rights, *The Human Rights Fact Sheet series*
(Available free of charge in English and French, on application to the Centre for Human Rights, UN Office at Geneva)
This series deals with selected questions of human rights that are under active consideration or are of particular interest. The series (with over 20 titles) offers an informed account of basic human rights, what the UN is doing to promote and protect them, and the international machinery available to help realise those rights. Titles include *The Rights of Indigenous Peoples, The Rights of the Child, The Committee on the Elimination of Racial Discrimination, Contemporary Forms of Slavery, Minority Rights, Discrimination Against Women: The Convention and the Committee,* and *Harmful Traditional Practices Affecting the Health of Women and Children.*

UNDP: *Human Development Report*
Oxford: Oxford University Press (available in several languages including Arabic, English, French, Spanish), 1995
Established in 1990, the *Human Development Report* is an annual publication focusing on a critical area of human development, such as the concept and measurement of human development, people's participation, and human security. The 1995 *Report* addresses gender disparities (in education, health, and employment), the nature and extent of male violence against women, and the inadequate representation of women in public life. Building on its Human Development Index (HDI) (the average achievement of a country in basic human capabilities), the 1995 *Report* introduces the Gender-related Development Index

(GDI) and the Gender Empowerment Measure (GEM), in order to disaggregate the HDI by sex. These dramatically demonstrate the extent to which women systematically fall below average achievement in terms of human development, throughout the industrialised and developing worlds. The findings of the *Report* also demonstrate that gender equity depends not on wealth, but on political commitment. The 1995 *Report* is unequivocal in placing gender equity at the heart of development: 'human development must be engendered. If development is meant to widen opportunities for all people, then continuing exclusion of women from many opportunities of life warps the process of development.'

UNESCO: *The Cultural Dimension of Development: Towards a Practical Approach*
Paris: UNESCO Culture and Development Series, 1995
This book explores what UNESCO considers to be the 'one important imponderable' in the development process which has yet to gain general recognition. This has to do with collective motivation of a community, which is, to a large extent, culturally determined, and which has to be mobilised if a development programme is to achieve more than mere economic growth and modernisation. The book represents a significant step towards developing some basic knowledge about the cultural factors that determine development. It is an attempt at a state-of-the-art presentation, based on experience gained both inside and outside the UN system, as well as a first outline of a possible methodology for integrating the cultural dimension into development programmes and projects.

UNHCR: *Refugee Children: Guidelines on Protection and Care*
Geneva: UNHCR, 1994 (available in English and French)
Fully revised to reflect the 1989 Convention on the Rights of the Child, and UNHCR's 1993 Policy on Refugee Children, the Guidelines outline principles and practice for the protection and assistance of refugee children.

Emphasis is given to children's developmental needs, their cultural context, the special requirements of unaccompanied minors, and issues arising from repatriation and reintegration.

UNICEF: *The State of the World's Children*
Oxford: Oxford University Press
An annual report on development through its impact on children. Supported by charts and statistical information, the report is not only a valuable source of information, but also offers critical analysis of development practice and policy from the perspective of children and their needs. Recent issues have focused on the need to eradicate 'the apartheid of gender', and on the devastating effect of 'pain now, gain later' macro-economic policies on the health and well-being of children and their families.

UNRISD: *Ethnic Conflict and Development*
Research Paper series, Geneva: UNRISD
Includes case-studies of 14 countries, in many of which ethnic diversity has been a component of violence. It examines the various forces that shape ethnicity, including economic factors; and shows the ways in which ethnicities are 'constructed', 'invented', and 'imagined' under specific circumstances.

UNRISD: *States of Disarray: The Social Effects of Globalisation*
Geneva: UNRISD (available in English, French, and Spanish), 1995
An examination of critical social problems such as poverty, unemployment, inequality, crime and drugs, and the themes of identity crisis, violent conflict, weakening of social solidarity, and the declining responsibility of public institutions. Part I discusses globalisation, in terms of its impact on impoverishment, inequalities, work insecurity, weakening of institutions and social support systems, and the erosion of established identities and values. Part II explores these developments in relation to crime, drugs, ethnic conflicts, and reconstruction of war-torn societies. Part III looks at the policy environment and the impact of the principal forces shaping contemporary

societies on a variety of institutions, stressing the links between misery and insecurity and social conflicts, including the rise of extremist movements.

UNRISD: *Technical Co-operation and Women's Lives: Integrating Gender into Development Planning*
Geneva: UNRISD, 1995
A research programme focusing on two critical themes: inequality in women's access to and participation in the definition of economic structures and policies and the productive process itself; and insufficient institutional mechanisms to promote the advancement of women. A series of ten papers by leading scholars assesses the efforts of major donor agencies (such as the World Bank, the ILO, and UNDP) and governments to integrate gender issues into their activities; including case-studies of Bangladesh, Jamaica, Morocco, Uganda, and Vietnam.

The Universal Declaration of Human Rights (1948)
(Available free of charge, in several languages, from the UN Department of Public Information, New York)
Adopted and proclaimed by the General Assembly of the UN on 10 December 1948, this is the clearest and most authoritative statement of the principle upon which most development and humanitarian relief work rests: that all human beings are born with equal and inalienable rights and fundamental freedoms. The Declaration is legally binding on member states of the United Nations. Subsequent Conventions, such as the Indigenous and Tribal People's Convention and the International Convention on the Elimination of All Forms of Discrimination Against Women, have to be ratified individually by each member state.

Werner, David: *Disabled Village Children*
Palo Alto: Hesperian Foundation, 1987
This is a book of ideas and information for all who are concerned about the well-being of disabled children, especially those who live in rural areas or are involved with community-based programmes. It gives a wealth of clear, simple, but detailed information covering the most common disabilities of children. It also gives suggestions for simplified rehabilitation, low-cost aids, and ways to help disabled children find a role and be accepted in the community. Above all, it stresses that most answers for meeting these children's needs can be found within the community, the family, and in the children themselves.

Williams, Suzanne et al.: *The Oxfam Gender Training Manual*
Oxford: Oxfam (UK and Ireland), 1993
This resource book for gender and development trainers draws on the work of gender trainers all over the world. It offers tried and tested activities and handouts, gathered from a wide range of sources in Africa, Asia, and Latin America and shaped into a coherent training programme. The manual includes activities which explore gender-awareness and self-awareness; gender roles and needs; gender-sensitive appraisal and planning; gender and major global issues, strategies for change.

Women and Development Series (1989-95)
London: Zed Books
Prepared under the direction of the UN NGO Liaison Service, a series consisting of ten volumes which focus on women and each of the following: human rights; empowerment; refugees; employment; literacy; the family; health; disability; world economic crisis; the environment. Provides a detailed overview of women's exclusion from the benefits of development, and of ways in which women's organisations and NGOs around the world, as well as the UN system, have attempted to 'mainstream' women's rights.

Journals

Ageing and Society (ISSN 0144-686X)
(published quarterly by Cambridge University Press)
Editor: Peter G Coleman, University of Southampton, UK
An international journal devoted to publishing contributions to the understanding of human ageing, particularly from the social and behavioural sciences and humanities. Its interpretation of ageing is wide and includes all aspects of the human condition, whether they relate to individuals, groups, societies, or institutions.

Ageways
Editor: Alison Tarrant
A quarterly news pack produced by HelpAge International, covering the organisation's work around the world, and issues relating to ageing and development.

Gender and Development (ISSN 1355-2074)
(published three times a year by Oxfam (UK and Ireland)
Editor: Caroline Sweetman, Oxfam (UK/I)
Each issues focuses on a specific theme relevant to gender and development issues, exploring the links between gender and development initiatives, and making links between theoretical and practical work in this field.

Journal of Cross-cultural Gerontology
(published quarterly by Kluwer Academic Publishers, The Netherlands) s
Editors: Cynthia M. Beall and Melvyn C. Goldstein, Case Western Reserve University, Cleveland, USA
An international and interdisciplinary journal providing a forum for scholarly discussions of the ageing process and the problems of the aged throughout the world. The journal emphasises discussions of research findings, theoretical issues, and applied approaches dealing with non-Western populations, but also invites articles that provide comparative orientation for the study of the ageing process in its social, economic, historical, and biological perspectives.

International Children's Rights Monitor
(ISSN: 0259 3696)
Editor: Paulo David
A quarterly publication of Defence for Children International, an independent NGO which seeks to ensure systematic and concerted international action to protect the rights of the child. *International Children's Rights Monitor*, produced in three language editions, is DCI's major tool for making known problems and responses in the children's rights field.

IRED Forum
Editors: Laurence Dumay and Fernand Vincent
A quarterly bulletin containing information and resources from the worldwide network IRED (Innovations et réseaux pour le développement). Published in English, French, and Spanish.

ISIS International
An international non-governmental women's organisation, founded in 1974 to promote the empowerment of women through information-sharing, communication, and networking. Isis International in Asia publishes the quarterly magazine *Women in Action*. ISIS International in Latin America coordinates a health network for Latin America and the Caribbean, for which it publishes the *Women's Health Journal*. ISIS in Africa publishes *Women's World* and coordinates the Women's International Cross Cultural Exchange. All three offices run an information and documentation centre.

Minority Rights Group
Publishes well researched and authoritative reports on particular minority groups all over the world, and on key issues, such as Minorities and Human Rights Law; International Action against Genocide; the Social Psychology of Minorities.

Race and Class (ISSN 0306-3968)
Editor: A Sivanandan
A journal for Black and Third World liberation published quarterly by the Institute of Race Relations, UK.

Signs (ISSN 0097 9740)
Editors: Ruth-Ellen Boetcher-Joeres and
Barbara Laslett
A journal of women in culture and society,
published quarterly by the University of
Chicago Press.

Survival International
Publishes a number of reports, documents, and
regular reviews on the situation of indigenous
peoples and ethnic minorities around the
world.

Vox Nostra
Newsletter/journal published quarterly by
Disabled People's International, in several
languages, including Arabic.

Publishers' addresses

Beacon Press, 25 Beacon Street, Boston, MA
02108-2892, USA

Cambridge University Press, The Edinburgh
Building, Shaftesbury Road, Cambridge CB2
2RU, UK

Centre for Human Rights, UN Office at
Geneva, 8-14 avenue de la Paix, 1211 Geneva
10, Switzerland

Chapman and Hall, 2-6 Boundary Row,
London SE1 8HN, UK

Defence for Children International, PO Box
88, 1211 Geneva, Switzerland

Disabled People's International, 101-7
Evergreen Place, Winnipeg, Manitoba,
Canada R3L 2T3

Earthscan, 120 Pentonville Road, London N1
9JN, UK

HelpAge International, St James's Walk,
London EC1R 0BE, UK

Hesperian Foundation, PO Box 1692, Palo
Alto, CA 94302, USA

Institute of Race Relations, 2-6 Leeke Street,
Kings Cross Road, London WC1X 9HS, UK

IRED, 3 rue de varembé, 1211 Geneva,
Switzerland
ISIS International, PO Box 1837, Quezon
City, Main Quezon City 1100, The Philippines

ISIS International, Casilla 2067, Correo
Central, Santiago, Chile

ISIS-WICCE, Box 4934, Kampala, Uganda

Kluwer Academic Publishers, Spuiboulevard
50, PO Box 17, 3300 AA Dordrecht, The
Netherlands

Minority Rights Group, 379 Brixton Road,
London SW9 7DE, UK

Monthly Review Press, 122 West 27th Street,
New York, NY 10001, USA

Oxfam (UK and Ireland), 274 Banbury Road,
Oxford OX2 7DZ, UK

Oxford University Press, Walton Street,
Oxford OX2 6DP, UK

Routledge, 11 New Fetter Lane, London,
EC4P 4EE, UK

Survival International, 11-15 Emerald Street,
London WC1N 3QL, UK

UN Department of Public Information, United
Nations, New York, NY 10017, USA

UNESCO, 7 place de Fontenoy, 75700 Paris,
France

UNHCR, Centre William Rappard, 154 rue de
Lausanne, 1202 Geneva, Switzerland

UNRISD, Palais des Nations, 1211 Geneva, Switzerland]

UN University Press, Toho Shimei Building, 15-1 Shibuya 2-chome, Shibuya-ku, Tokyo 150, Japan

United States Institute of Peace Press, 1550 M Street NW, Washington DC 20005, USA

University of Chicago Press, Journals Division, 5720 S. Woodlawn, Chicago, IL 60637, USA

University of Pennsylvania Press, 418 Service Drive, Philadelphia, PA 19104-6097, USA
Verso Press, 6 Meard Street, London W1V 3HR, UK

Westview Press, 5500 Central Avenue, Boulder, Colorado 80301-2877, USA

Zed Books, 9 Cynthia Street, London N1 9JF, UK

Oxfam Publications

Oxfam (UK and Ireland) publishes a wide range of books, manuals, journals, and resource materials for specialist, academic, and general readers. For a free catalogue, please write to

Oxfam Publishing
274 Banbury Road
Oxford OX2 7DZ, UK

telephone 01865 311311
e-mail publish@oxfam.org.uk

Oxfam publications are available from the following agents:
for Canada and the USA: Humanities Press International, 165 First Avenue, Atlantic Highlands, New Jersey NJ 07716-1289, USA; tel. (908) 872 1441; fax (908) 872 0717
for southern Africa: David Philip Publishers, PO Box 23408, Claremont, Cape Town 7735, South Africa; tel. (021) 64 4136; fax (021) 64 3358.